ARMENIANS IN THE SERVICE OF
THE OTTOMAN EMPIRE
1860-1908

ZENO
Booksellers & Publishers
(The Greek Bookshop)
6 DENMARK STREET
LONDON WC2H 8LP
TEL: (071) 836 2522

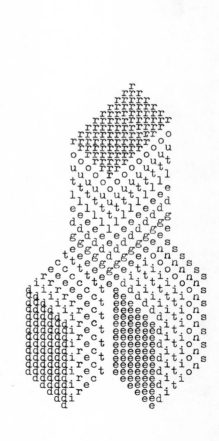

ARMENIANS IN THE SERVICE OF THE OTTOMAN EMPIRE 1860-1908

MESROB K. KRIKORIAN

ROUTLEDGE DIRECT EDITIONS

ROUTLEDGE & KEGAN PAUL
London, Henley and Boston

First published in 1977
by Routledge & Kegan Paul Ltd
39 Store Street,
London WC1E 7DD,
Broadway House,
Newtown Road,
Henley-on-Thames,
Oxon RG9 1EN and
9 Park Street,
Boston, Mass. 02108, USA
Printed by Thomson Litho Ltd
East Kilbride, Scotland
© Mesrob K. Krikorian 1977

British Library Cataloguing in Publication Data

Krikorian, Mesrob K
Armenians in the service of the Ottoman
Empire, 1860-1908.
1. Armenians in Turkey 2. Armenians in Syria
I. Title
301.45'19'19920566   DR435.A7   77-30080

ISBN 0-7100-8564-8

Owing to production delays
this book was published in 1978

CONTENTS

PREFACE

Hundreds of books have been written on the Armenian Question and massacres, yet very little is known about the services of Armenians in the cultural, economic and administrative life and development of the Ottoman Empire. This study is an investigation into the contribution by Armenians to the Ottoman public life, especially in Eastern Anatolia and Syria from 1860 when the Armenian community in Turkey was given a new legislative Constitution on the basis of 'Tanzimat' (reforms), until 1908 when the Young Turks seized the power and followed a bitter fanatic national-religious policy which had tragic consequences for both the Armenians and Turks.

I have deliberately limited the area of investigation to the eastern provinces of Anatolia which earlier formed the western part of historic Armenia and which in the diplomatic language of the nineteenth century (until the Treaty signed at Sèvres, 10 August 1920) was referred to as 'provinces inhabited by Armenians'. To these 'vilâyets' I have added the provinces of Syria which neighboured the Armenian Kingdom of Cilicia and where, especially in and round Aleppo, old Armenian communities had settled. Both in Anatolia and Syria, the Armenians were employed in various administrative, judicial, economic and secretarial fields and, to a lesser extent, in technical affairs, agriculture, education and public health. And this in spite of the fact that, for the Armenians, these were forty-eight years of transition from established status of a favoured Christian 'millet' to the tragic insecurity of a hunted people.

This study is necessarily based on the Ottoman provincial yearbooks ('salname') which recorded in detail the names, ranks and functions of the paid officials and unpaid community representatives and private citizens who served the numerous local bodies. In 1263 H/1846-7 the Ottoman Empire began to publish imperial year-books ('Devlet-i âliye-i osmaniye salnamesi'), listing the officials of the central and provincial governments (S.R. Iskit, 'Türkiyede neşriyat hareketleri tarihine bir bakiş' ('A Historical Survey of Publishing Activities in Turkey'), Istanbul, 1939, pp.34-6 and 356-61 and 'EI' 1st, iv, p.83). In 1284H/1867-8 the chief secretary ('mektubcu') of the province of Aleppo, Ibrahim Halet Bey (a biography of whom can be seen in 'Türkiye Ansiklopedisi' ('Encyclopaedia of Turkey'),

Ankara, iii, 1956, p.133) published a statistical annual of the province. Soon other 'vilâyets' followed the example of Aleppo, and
thus there were created the provincial year-books (Iskit, op. cit.,
pp.96-7). These 'salnames' gave the geography, produce, population
and all the officials and officers of their provinces. As Iskit has
pointed out in an exaggerated way the 'vilâyet-salnames' are 'for
the most part wrong' (ibid., pp.360-1), but in my research, mis-
spellings of names, and also mistakes in geographical and historical
surveys did not cause any special difficulty, because I was inter-
ested in differentiating between the names of the Muslim and Christian officials, while compiling statistics of personnel of all the
departments of government affairs.

In Europe the best collection of the provincial year-books of
Eastern Anatolia is possessed by the Bibliothèque Nubar of the
Armenian General Benevolent Union in Paris. In order to study a
sufficient number of these 'salnames' for comparative purposes, I
undertook a tour of the Middle East and worked in the Library of the
American University of Beirut, in the State Library of Aleppo, and
in the libraries of the University and of the Municipality of
Istanbul. The last ('Istanbul Belediye Kütübhanesi') has quite a
large collection of year-books.

At the beginning of each chapter I have made a historical survey
of the relevant province. For this part of my study I have con-
sulted the 'Encyclopaedia of Islâm' (first and second editions),
'Islâm Ansiklopedisi', Ş. Fraşeri's 'Qâmûs ül-a'lâm' ('Dictionary of
Proper Names'), R. Grousset's 'Histoire de l'Arménie', Y. Manandian's 'Critical Survey of the History of the Armenian People',
M. Ormanian's 'History of the Armenian Nation', local histories of
the Armenian communities in Eastern Anatolia and Syria, and other
sources which are referred to as they occur. In presenting the administrative structure of the 'vilâyets', I have utilized the imperial and provincial year-books, the encyclopaedias mentioned
above, and 'La Turquie d'Asie' of V. Cuinet. In order to enable the
reader to locate the place names of Eastern Anatolia on modern maps,
I have adopted the renderings as given in the gazetteer of Turkey
('Türkiyede meskûn yerler kilavuzu' ('Gazetteer of the Inhabited
Places of Turkey'), published by the Ministry of the Interior of
Turkey, Ankara, two volumes, 1946-7), except that for technical
reasons instead of the guttural consonant 'ğ' I have written 'gh' or
simply 'g'.

At the end of each chapter I have appended selected biographies
of those Armenians who acted in Ottoman public life for a long
period or held comparatively high positions in the government. I
have drawn these biographies from local Armenian histories. The
provincial year-books in this case were of little help, since the
officials are very often referred to only by their Christian names.
These biographies will serve to give the reader a more substantial
idea of the participation of the Armenian community in Ottoman
public life.

ACKNOWLEDGMENTS

In 1958 while lecturing on Armenian history, classical language and literature at the Hovaguimian-Manouguian High School in Beirut, I was offered a scholarship for three years by the Calouste Gulbenkian Foundation in order to propagate interest in Armenian studies at the University of Durham. Because of the civil war I could not leave Lebanon immediately, but in January 1959 I went to England and was received warmly by St John's College at Durham. The Principal, Mr J.P. Hickinbotham MA, Mr John Cockerton MA and my other friends helped me in every way: I thank all of them for their wonderful hospitality. I am particularly grateful to the Director of the School of Oriental Studies, Professor T.W. Thacker who encouraged me to undertake research about the service of the Armenians in the Ottoman Empire. I am much indebted also to Professor Richard Hill who kindly accepted me as a special student in the Modern History of the Middle East and agreed to be my supervisor. During the years from 1959 to 1963 he was very helpful in reading my book and making useful suggestions. While working as a post-graduate research-fellow in Armenian Studies at the University of Durham, I improved my Modern and Ottoman Turkish, as well as my Arabic, with assistance of the late Mr C.G. Simpson, Reader in Turkish at the University of Durham, and of Professor F.R.C. Bagley, Reader in Arabic and Persian: I express my gratitude to them! I acknowledge my debt also to Mr I.J.C. Foster MA, the former Keeper of Oriental Books at the University of Durham, who provided for me rare books from all parts of the world. It is a pleasant duty for me now to give my heartfelt thanks to all, among them Messrs Nerses Zohrab and Sarkis Karabetian from Vienna, who wished to see my work published in form of a book. I would like to make mention here again of the trustees of the Calouste Gulbenkian Foundation for their generous scholarship. I sincerely thank my nephew Mr Azad Ajamian who presented and recommended my book to Routledge & Kegan Paul Ltd. My deepest thanks of course go to one of my best friends, Dr Aram B. Davoudians of Meshed/Iran who, in memoriam of his late father Babadjan, nobly offered the necessary subsidy for the publication of my research; may God bless the good memory of all members of Davoudians' family who sleep and repose in eternal peace.

Vienna, 1976   M.K.K.

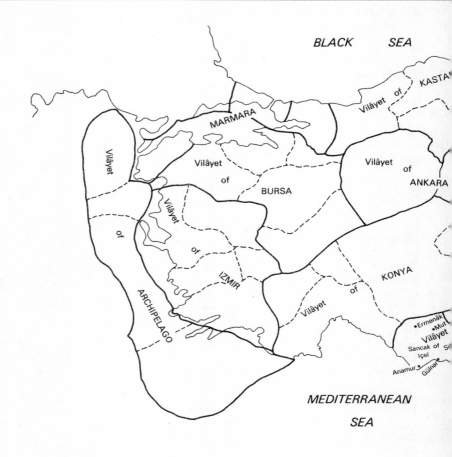

BLACK SEA

Vilâyet of KASTA...

Vilâyet

Vilâyet
of
BURSA

MARMARA

Vilâyet
of
ANKARA

Vilâyet
of

Vilâyet
of
IZMIR

KONYA

ARCHIPELAGO

Vilâyet
of

•Ermenâk
•Mut
Vilâyet
Sancak of Si...
İçel
Anamur• •Gülnar

MEDITERRANEAN

SEA

AN ADMINISTRATIVE MAP

OF

ANATOLIA AND SYRIA

(Second half of the XIXth Century)

0   50 100 150 200 km

Scale: 1:6,000,000

■ = Centres
• = Outer districts

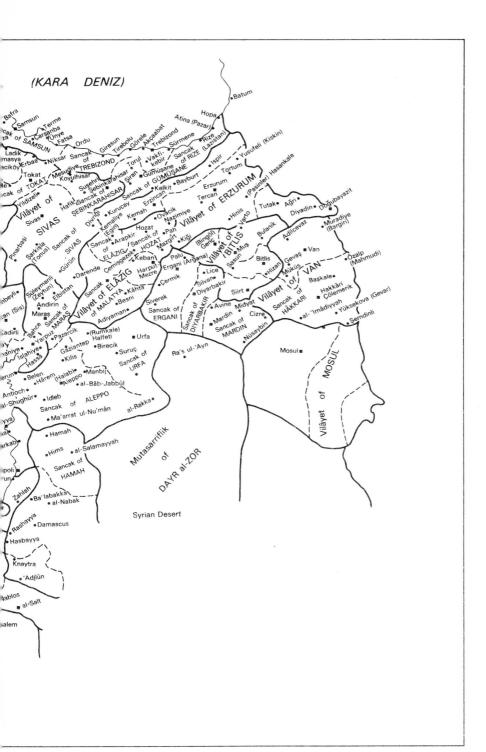

(KARA DENIZ)

Batum

Bafra
Samsun
Terme
Carşanba
Ünye
Fatsa
cak of SAMSUN
Ordu
Giresun
Tirebolu
Görele
Akçaabat
Trebizond
Sürmene
Rize
Atina (Pazar)
Hopa
Ladik
masya
acıköy
Erbaa
Niksar
Sancak
of
TREBIZOND
Vakfı-
kebir
Torul
Sancak of
RIZE (Lazistan)
Yusufeli (Kiskin)
Tokat
Mesudiye
Susehri
Koyulhisar
Sebinkarahisar
Şiran
Gümüsane
Kelkit
Bayburt
Erzurum
İspir
Tortum
Tercan
Sancak of
TOKAT
Hafik
Sancak of
SEBINKARAHISAR
Sancak of GÜMÜSANE
Yıldızeli
Vilâyet of
SIVAS
Divriği
Kemaliye
(Egin)
Kemah
Erzincan
Ovacik
Nazimiye
Vilâyet of ERZURUM
(Pasinler) Hasankale
Sivas
Kurucay
Arapkir
Hozat
Pah
Hinis
Varto
Tutak
Ağrı
Diyadin
Doğubayazit
Pinarbaşi
Sarkisla
(Tonus)
Sancak of
SIVAS
Sancak of
ELAZIG
of
Sancak of
HOZAT
Mazgirt
Kiğı
(Bingöl)
Genç
Vilâyet of
BITLIS
Bulanik
Muradiye
(Bargiri)
Gürün
Cemişgezek
Keban
Palu
Ergani (Argana)
Sasun
Muş
Van
Adilcevaz
Özalp
(Mahmudi)
Darende
Harput-
Mezre
Bitlis
Gevaş
Müküs
Süleymanli
(Zeytun)
Elbistan
Vilâyet of ELAZIG
Kâhta
Çermik
Lice
Hizan
Vilâyet of
VAN
Başkale
Andirin
Sancak of
MALATYA
Besni
Silvan
Diyarbakir
Siirt
Sancak of
HAKKARI
Hakkâri
Çölemerik
Maraş
Adiyaman
Siverek
Sancak of
Avine
Midyat
al-'Imâdiyyah
Yüksekova (Gevar)
beyli
(Sis)
Bahce
Yarpuz
Pazarcik
Siverek
ERGANI
Sancak of
DIYARBAKIR
Mardin
Cizre
Nüsaybin
Semdinli
adirli
haniye
Islahiye
Hassa
Gaziantep
(Rumkale)
Halfeti
Birecik
Sancak of
MARDIN
erun
Belen
Hârem
Kilis
Suruç
Urfa
Ra's ul-'Ayn
Mosul
Vilâyet of MOSUL
(Halab)
Manbij
Sancak of
URFA
Antioch
al-Shughûr
Idleb
Sancak
of
ALEPPO
al-Bâb-Jabbûl
al-Rakka
yya
Hamah
Ma'arrat ul-Nu'mân
Mutasarriflik
of
DAYR al-ZOR
arkab
Hims
al-Salamayyah
Sancak of
HAMAH
poli
Zahlah
Ba'labakka
al-Nabak
Syrian Desert
Rashayya
Damascus
Hasbayya
Knaytra
'Adjlûn
ablos
al-Salt
salem

ABBREVIATIONS

Arm.	Armenian
Arb.	Arabic
'CTA'	V. Cuinet, 'La Turquie d'Asie'
'EI' 1st	'The Encyclopaedia of Islâm', first edition
'EI' 2nd	'The Encyclopaedia of Islâm', second edition
FO	Foreign Office, London
'IA'	'Islâm Ansiklopedisi'
Mod.Turk.	Modern Turkish
Ott.Turk.	Ottoman Turkish
PRO	Public Record Office, London

INTRODUCTION

THE SCOPE OF THIS WORK

The participation of the Armenian community in Ottoman public life
in Eastern Anatolia and Syria has not been as yet a subject of
particular research. There are numerous studies on the political,
religious and cultural history of the Armenians of Anatolia and
Syria, but there is no special study in any language on their
participation in Ottoman public life.

In Turkish sources the role which the Armenians played in Ottoman
governmental affairs has been intentionally ignored, and even
Armenian sources have paid little attention to it. To the Armenian
mind a churchman or a man of letters tends to be more appreciated
and better remembered than a humdrum administrator in a district or
province. This is the reason why the local histories of Anatolia
and Syria, written by Armenian scholars, contain little material on
the biographies of those who served in the different departments of
the Ottoman Government.

In 1953, at Istanbul, Y. Çark published an illustrated book,
'Türk devleti hizmetinde Ermeniler, 1453-1953' ('The Armenians in
the Service of the Turkish State, 1453-1953'), in which he recorded
those Armenians who held more or less important positions in the
Turkish State from 1453 to 1953. In point of time this study covers
a period of five centuries and, geographically, the whole Ottoman
Empire up to 1923 and the Turkish Republic thereafter. Second, the
book related not what the Armenians, taken as a community, have
achieved, but what individual Armenians have done in the Turkish
service. Moreover, the author has not produced any new information,
but has been content to compile only well-known printed material.
Only at pages 168-79 of his compilation does he mention the names of
some of the Armenians who took part in Ottoman public life in
Eastern Anatolia and Syria.

My main sources in writing the present work have been the provincial year-books of Eastern Anatolia and Syria. Although these
are printed or lithographed books, the fact that they are scarce and
not much explored gives them the character of unedited materials.

The service of the Armenians to the central government of the
Ottoman Empire in and around Istanbul is known to some extent. This

1

is the reason why I have chosen as geographical limits that part of
Anatolia which was called in the West 'Turkish Armenia' and which
was considered in western diplomacy to be 'provinces inhabited by
Armenians'; and Syria, where the Armenians began to settle as early
as the twelfth century, and which since the fourteenth century included the important See of Aleppo of the Armenian Cilician
Catholicate.

Chronologically, this work covers the period between 1860 and
1908. The year 1860 is significant in Armenian-Ottoman history for
several reasons: (a) On 3 November 1839 the 'Hatti şerif' (noble
rescript) of Sultan Abdülmecid (which was reaffirmed on 18 February
1856 by the 'Hatti hümayun' = Imperial rescript), proclaimed freedom
of worship and civil equality to all Ottoman subjects. As a result
of these imperial edicts non-Muslims were admitted in greater
numbers than before to employment in the Ottoman public administration.

(b) From 1857-8 onwards, the Armenians and other non-Muslim
students were also allowed to attend the Turkish state high schools.
Through this new arrangement Armenians enjoyed the opportunity of
learning advanced Turkish and various professions and skills and
were thus fitted to engage in public affairs. It must be mentioned
here that, apart from Turkish schools, the Armenians had their own
secondary schools, as well as others run by French Catholic and
American Protestant Missions which did much to develop popular education. Many Armenians, after leaving the local high schools, went
abroad, especially to Paris and New York, and, nearer home, to the
two colleges, later universities, of Beirut, in order to continue
their education. These two universities are the Syrian Protestant
College which was founded in 1866 by the American Presbyterian
Mission and became the American University of Beirut in 1920; and
the Jesuit College founded in 1881 (run by French Fathers), now the
University of Saint-Joseph. Most of the students returned home and
devoted themselves to public service and the private professions.

(c) In 1860 the Constitution of the Armenian community was first
promulgated. This stimulated a renaissance of education and literature in the national life and awakened the national conscience of
the younger generation.

(d) In 1860 occurred the massacres of the Maronites of Mount
Lebanon by the Druzes, and consequently Jabal Lubnân became an
autonomous territory guaranteed by international agreement.

(e) In October 1864 the Ottoman Empire was itself reorganized and
divided into reconstituted provinces ('vilâyet') under governors
designated 'vali'. This territorial reorganization created employment for many new officials in public life, for which the Armenians
and Greeks were now available.

My period ends in 1908-9 when the Young Turks came into power and
pursued a nationalistic policy which had its result in the extermi-
nation of the whole Armenian population from Anatolia in 1915-20,
bringing misery to Turk and Armenian alike.

There are hundreds of books on the Armenian Question and massacres but they emphasize one side of the story to the obscuring of
the other side and, accordingly, one can hardly imagine after reading this type of literature that Ottoman-Armenian co-operation ever
existed or that the Armenians had rendered a considerable service to

Ottoman public life. My work has been, therefore, to demonstrate the great part which the Armenians took in the public administration of Eastern Anatolia and Syria in the period of the 'Tanzimat' (reforms). It should be understood how much the three million Armenians of Anatolia contributed to the economy and general development of the country, apart from official service, through trade, agriculture, handicrafts and the professions.

THE REGULATION OF THE ARMENIAN COMMUNITY

The Armenians' way of life had distinctive features and their cultural and educational affairs were carried out in the main by clergymen, assisted by prominent laymen. The Armenian communities in the Ottoman Empire up to 1860 were governed by the Patriarch of Istanbul through councils in which the ordinary people had almost no representation.

On 11 'Cemaziyel âhir' 1272H (18 February 1856) the 'Hatti hümayun' (Imperial rescript) of the Sublime Porte proclaimed personal safety and freedom of worship to all Ottoman subjects without any distinction and promised to non-Muslim communities restoration of all immunities and privileges in a new legislative form. (1) Reform in the state suggested reform in the religious communities. The Armenians with all other non-Muslim communities were pleased and enthusiastic. Some intellectuals such as Krikor Odian (1834-87), Nahapet Russinian (1819-76) and Dr Serovbê Vitchênian (1815-87) who were educated in the secular environment of Paris, urged the necessity of a new constitution for the Armenian community in order to restrict the arbitrary acts of the patriarchs, 'âmirs' (high officials at the Court) and 'aghas' (chiefs, notables) and to give the ordinary people a say in the ordering of their communal life.

In the year 1856-7 a special committee led by Krikor Efendi Markosian drew up a draft regulation for the Armenian community. This was examined in February-March 1857 by the communal Supreme Assembly, and on 3 April 1857 was approved by the General Council. It was not, however, accepted by the Porte, because, it was said, 'no state can be within another state'. (2) The Armenians were thus compelled to prepare a new constitution which was completed in 1860. These were its main lines: (3)

1.   'Each individual has obligations towards the nation ['millet' = 'community'] and the nation towards the individual.' Every Armenian would participate in the elections of the patriarch and community councils through representatives and would pay taxes in order to preserve and defend his rights.

2.   The patriarch is no longer an omnipotent authority in the community, but merely 'the president of the communal councils', who also 'administered the executive power of these councils'.

3.   The supreme communal authority is the General Council with the power to elect the patriarch, to organize the community, to oversee and inspect the activities of the directorship of the councils and to preserve the Constitution.

4.   Next to the General Council are set up the Religious and Political Councils, the Boards of Education, Finance, Expenditure and Income, Social Litigation (concerning family disputes) and Parish Councils.

5.   The task of the Parish Council is to administer the local community affairs of the district, to maintain the church and the school, to settle the disputes which arise between the members of the Parish and to help the poor.

6.   In the provinces also, there would be Diocesan, Religious, Political and Parish Councils. Representatives of these councils and also other Armenians who held a respectable position in Ottoman public life, would form the General Council of each 'vilâyet'. The duty of the General Council is to elect the prelate, to organize the Religious and Political Councils, and to oversee the activities of the councils.

On 5 June 1860 representatives of all classes of the Armenian community met in General Council in Istanbul where the new Regulation was approved and signed and at the same time provisional councils were formed. A copy of the Constitution was submitted to the Sublime Porte for ratification; in three months new councils were elected and community life suddenly began to be administered according to the new regulations until 27 August 1861, when the execution of the Constitution was forbidden by the Ottoman Government. Again a special committee was appointed, this time by the Sublime Porte, under the chairmanship of Dr Serovbê Vitchênian (known as Dr Servitchên) which revised the Constitution and re-submitted it to the government in January 1862. On the suggestions of the government once more certain changes were made and the people awaited anxiously the ratification of the Constitution. (4)

It is of interest to note here the main points which were altered in the regulations:

1.   Some terms such as the council of 'National Administration', apparently regarded as suspicious by the government, were cut out or replaced by other words: e.g. in the 'Fundamental principles' instead of 'National Constitution' of articles iv and v, in the revised Constitutions the term is shortened to 'nation' (articles ii and iii). Again, in article v of the 'Fundamental principles' it was suggested that the 'National Administration' should not spare any labour for the reformation and progress of the nation; in the revised form it is said that 'the nation should devotedly work for the national progress' (article iii) and thus the dangerous word 'reformation' was omitted.   Article 27 also, 'The Political Council is composed of 20 political laymen' ('qaghaqagêt' = he who understands politics, a politician), because of the word 'political', is altered to this: 'The Political Council consists of 20 laymen well acquainted with the national affairs and with the laws of the Ottoman Empire' (article 36).

2.   In the revised Constitution all mention concerning the relations of the Armenian Patriarchate of Istanbul with the Holy See of Etchmiadzin in Russian Armenia is eradicated. In article 8 it was said that the National Administration 'in connection with the Araratean Mother See (= the Holy See of Etchmiadzin) would remain faithful to the same relations by which the Nation and the See were joined together from the beginning' and in article 115 appeared this: 'The patriarch should be ordained by the Catholicos of Etchmiadzin and should be an Ottoman subject.' These parts of the Constitution are omitted from the revised form and it is stated that the patriarch should be elected from the bishops who live in the

Ottoman Empire and who by birth are Ottoman subjects (articles 1-2).

3. According to the revised Constitution the election of the patriarch and of the Political and Religious Councils must be 'affirmed by Imperial order', whereas previously only the election of the patriarch was to be presented to the Porte for approval.

4. In the revised Constitution a special section (articles 17-23) is added concerning the election of the Armenian patriarch of Jerusalem.

The government did not immediately confirm even the revised Constitution. The people, thinking that the Patriarchate was delaying the matter, organized demonstrations. Eventually by a decree dated 9 'Şevval' 1279H (30 March 1863) the Sultan Abdül'aziz approved the Community Regulation which was handed over to the patriarchal locum tenens, Bishop Stephan Maghachian, by the Grand Vizier Mehmed Emin Ali Paşa. It is worth noting that, although the Armenians had their new Regulation called 'National Constitution' (Arm. 'Azgayin Sahmanadruthiwn'), the Turkish text was entitled 'Regulation of the Armenian Nation' ('Nizamname-i millet-i ermenian'), whereas in 'Düstûr' (5) it was named 'The Regulation of the Armenian Patriarchate' ('Ermeni patrikligi nizamati'). These differences in the title of the Armenian Constitution help us to observe the differences between the Armenian and Turkish attitudes to the national status. While the Armenians thought that the new Constitution would bring secularism, internal freedom and safety to their lives, to the Turks the Armenian population of the Ottoman Empire, like the other non-Muslim peoples, in spite of promised or written reforms, were still treated as a religious community, a 'millet' (6) and were recognized and treated only through their religious organization. However, it is a fact that the Constitution basically organized the Armenian community, limited the power of the patriarch and of lay despots, stimulated learning among the people, and thus became one of the main factors which resulted in a renaissance of literature among the Armenians of Turkey.

In the days of patriarch Malachia Ormanian, the Constitution was suspended from 1898 to 1906, because the Sultan Abdülhamid demanded a new revision of it. In 1923, in the creation of Turkish republic it became invalid, since all the Ottoman legislation ceased to be valid.

RUSSO-TURKISH WAR AND THE TREATY OF SAN STEFANO

No historical phenomenon or event can be precisely represented without the background of political life of the time. In order to show the difficult conditions under which the Armenian community of Eastern Anatolia took part in Ottoman public life from 1860 to 1908, it will be necessary only to list some of the principal external events: the Russo-Turkish War, the Treaty of San Stefano, the Congress of Berlin and the Ottoman Reforms proposed by the Powers.

For nearly four centuries the Armenians of Eastern Anatolia were oppressed under Ottoman rule. Especially in the provinces of Van, Bitlis and Erzurum, far from the control of the central government and at the mercy of Kurdish and Turkish petty despots and local thieves, the Armenian population was much maltreated. In 1876 the

Armenian Patriarchate at Istanbul published a report (7) based on
material from its archives, in which the sufferings of the Armenians
of the Eastern provinces were brought to the attention of the
public.

On 31 March 1877, the Powers drafted an agreed project of reform
respecting the countries and peoples under the Ottoman rule and submitted it to the Sublime Porte.   On 9 April 1877 the Ottoman Government rejected the project.   Russia undertook military action and
marched into the Ottoman territories.   Turkey asked for an armistice
to which Russia agreed and negotiations for a treaty were held at
Adrianople.   The Armenian prelate of Adrianople, Kevork Rusdjuklian,
together with Yovhannes Efendi Nurian and Stephan Arslanian (both of
them men of distinction from Istanbul), on the suggestion of the
Armenian Patriarchate and 'National Council' at Istanbul, presented
the Armenian Question to the Grand Duke Nicholas, the Russian Commander, and to Count Ignatiev, a Russian statesman and former consul
at Istanbul, asking them for reforms in the Eastern provinces.   The
Russians promised that the treaty in preparation would include the
following clause in favour of Armenians:

> For the purpose of preventing the oppressions and atrocities which
> have occurred in the Ottoman Empire's European and Asiatic
> provinces, the Sultan guarantees, in agreement with the Czar, to
> grant administrative local self-government to the provinces in-
> habited by Armenians (Van, Bitlis, Erzurum, Diyarbakir, Elâzig
> and Sivas). (8)

When the Russian delegates came to San Stefano (now Yeşil Köy near
the Istanbul airport, west of the city) and resided at the house of
an Armenian notable named Araqel Bey Dadian, the Armenian patriarch
Nerses Varjapetian went personally and besought Count Ignatiev to
insist on the urgency of the reforms affecting the Armenians of
Eastern Anatolia.

On 3 March 1878 the Russians and the Turks signed a treaty of
peace in San Stefano, granting favours to Montenegro, Serbia,
Bosnia, Herzogovina and especially to Bulgaria which would consti-
tute an autonomous tributary under a Christian government and with a
national militia.   Article xvi of the treaty also was a guarantee
for the reforms in 'the provinces inhabited by the Armenians', as
follows:

> As the evacuation by the Russian troops of the territory which
> they occupy in Armenia and which is to be restored to Turkey,
> might give rise to conflicts and complications detrimental to the
> maintenance of good relations between the two countries (Russia
> and Turkey), the Sublime Porte engages to carry into effect,
> without further delay, the improvements and reforms demanded by
> local requirements in the provinces inhabited by Armenians and to
> guarantee their security against the Kurds and Circassians. (9)

The Armenians at that time were enthusiastic and hopeful that after
long centuries they would again have, if not complete independence,
a semi-independence or local Christian administration in their homeland, like the Christians of the Lebanon.   It was, however, in-
genuous of them to expect any independence or even reform, because,
first, they lacked a resolute Power to protect them and, second, the
eastern frontier of Anatolia, particularly the fortress of Erzurum,
had great strategic importance.   A Turkish document which survives

in French translation in the Public Record Office, London, 'Resumé
de différents mémoirs spéciaux concernant notre arrangement défensif
au théâtre de la guerre arménienne', illuminates the matter.   This
document is the report of the meetings of an assembly (1858-60),
under the presidency of Selim Paşa, which planned in detail how to
defend the Empire in case of a Russian attack.   It is said there,
that Armenia and Asia Minor are the body of the Ottoman State, while
other Ottoman regions form its members, and that Erzurum is the most
important centre from which the body could be defended:
> Ce qui le centre du théâtre de la guerre, le point auquel toutes
> les routes mentionées se réunissent, la ville d'Erzeroum, soit
> fortifiée à grande échelle, comme pivot et dépôt général pour
> toutes nos forces.   La dite capitale, est, pour ainsi dire, la
> clef de l'espace à défendre, puisqu'elle domine toutes les
> communications importantes qui y aboutissent comme au point de
> noeud naturel. (10)
From this statement it can clearly be seen that any demand for in-
dependence or reform by Armenians in or around the province of
Erzurum would inevitably meet with the resistance of the Turks.

THE CONGRESS OF BERLIN

The European Powers, particularly England and Austria, were dis-
contented with the Treaty of San Stefano.   The Prime Minister of
Great Britain, Lord Beaconsfield, commented in the House of Lords
that by the Treaty of San Stefano European dominions were put under
the Russian administration and that the Black Sea was to be a
Russian lake as much as the Caspian.   Lord Salisbury also expressed
his view on the subject that the Russian Government by the Treaty of
San Stefano would be 'dominant over the vicinity of the Black Sea';
Armenians would fall under the immediate influence of Russia, while
the extensive European trade, passing from Trebizond to Persia,
would be 'liable to be arrested at the pleasure of the Russian
Government by the prohibitory barriers of their commerical system'.
(11)
   The Ottoman Government itself was not at all happy with the
Treaty of San Stefano.   The Armenians, being Christians like the
Russians and having a part of their country under Russian domina-
tion, especially after the Russo-Turkish War, were much suspected of
being Russian agents.   For this reason Turkey strongly endeavoured
to reject the Russian troops, who were to guarantee the execution of
the administrative reforms in Eastern Anatolia.
   From 13 June to 13 July 1878, Russia was urged by the European
Powers to attend the Congress of Berlin to reconsider the Treaty of
San Stefano.   An Armenian delegation, composed of Meguerditch
Kherimian (former patriarch and the archbishop of Beşiktaş in
Istanbul), archbishop Khorên Nar Bey and the two lay deputies from
the Armenian National Council of Istanbul, Minas Tcheraz and Stephan
Papazian, went to Berlin and submitted a letter to the Congress
together with a project for the reorganization of Turkish Armenia,
in which they said:
> Nous ne réclamons donc pas de liberté politique et nous ne
> voulons nullement nous séparer du Gouvernement Turc.   Nous

voulons seulement avoir dans une partie de l'Arménie Turque,
c'est-à-dire dans les 'vilâyets' d'Erzeroum et de Van et dans la
partie septentrionale du 'vilâyet' de Diyarbakir (v. la carte ci-
jointe) où nous avons la majorité sur les Turcs, conformement aux
documents statistiques ci-inclus, nous voulons avoir, disons nous,
un 'vali' armenien nommé par la S. Porte avec l'assentiment des
Puissances. Ce 'vali' sera chargé de l'administration locale
pour un temps déterminé; il devra disposer d'une police pour
maintenir l'ordre et la securité, et d'une partie des revenus du
pays, pour en assurer le developpement moral et matériel. (12)
Apparently the Armenian Question was affected by the conflict between the Powers. Turkey was afraid of the partition of her
dominions; the Western Powers were pursuing only their own interests, while Russia this time was not insistent in respect of the
Armenian problem. Consequently article xvi of the Treaty of San
Stefano was one of the articles tampered with at the Congress of
Berlin in favour of the Turks. It was pushed back to the end of the
new treaty, as article lxi, and direct Russian supervision was ex-
changed for the oversight of six Powers. This is the full text of
the article:
    Improvements and reforms in favour of Armenians. Protection
    against Circassians and Kurds. The Powers to be kept
    periodically informed.
       Art. LXI. The Sublime Porte undertakes to carry out, without
    further delay, the improvements and reforms demanded by local
    requirements in the provinces inhabited by the Armenians and to
    guarantee their security against the Circassians and Kurds. It
    will periodically make known the steps taken to this effect to
    the Powers, who will superintend their application. (13)
    The Armenian delegates who were not allowed even to enter the
building of the Congress, returned home dejected, having lost what
was already gained through the Treaty of San Stefano. They realized
that there was no room for any religion or pity in diplomacy and
that in politics self-interest and strength are always triumphant.
M. Kherimian on his return to Istanbul allegorically expressed his
conclusions on the Congress of Berlin thus:
    All the dominions came to the Congress with iron spoons and took
    their share of the 'harisa' [an oriental dish, cooked with meat
    and wheat and pounded together]. Since our spoon [i.e. the
    letter] was of paper, we could not get any of it. (14)
The Armenian intellectuals at Istanbul and in Anatolia were disappointed by the Treaty of Berlin, but the Armenian masses were
enthusiastic and active. In 1880 the 'United Society' (Miatseal
Enkeruthiwn') and other societies were organized to sponsor schools
in Turkish Armenia and to stimulate education and literature in the
new generation.

THE MASSACRES OF 1894-6 AND THE ADMINISTRATIVE REFORMS OF 1896

The administrative reforms, which by the Treaty of Berlin the
Sublime Porte promised to the European Powers for the 'provinces
inhabited by Armenians' in Anatolia, were not executed for more than
fifteen years. The Armenians being disappointed protested and

demonstrated, but this was unwise. The Porte, instead of fulfilling
the promises, grew obdurate, and, as it were by a coincidence,
massive massacres broke out in the Asian part of the Empire. The
'valis' and the army, aided by the Kurds, killed thousands of
Armenians in Anatolia, and many houses, shops and other properties
of the Armenians were destroyed or robbed. The first echo in
England of the Armenian massacres was a short report in 'The Times'
of 21 February 1894 on the troubles in Yozgat.

In March 1894 H.F.B. Lynch, who had just returned to England from
his tour of Armenia, in a letter addressed to the editor of 'The
Times', criticized the oppressive policy and the hostile treatment
of Armenians by the Turks in Eastern Anatolia and concluded thus:
> Unless our diplomacy is able to persuade the Porte that in
> pursuing their present policy towards the Armenians they are
> digging the grave of their Empire in Asia, the consequences are
> likely to be momentous not only for Turkey but for ourselves.
> (15)

The European States unfortunately could not stop the massacres
which continued in the years 1895 and 1896 throughout Anatolia. The
correspondent of 'The Times' in Turkey reported on the results of
the troubles as follows:
> They [the Armenians] are considerably reduced in numbers; there
> are thousands of helpless widows among them, and tens of
> thousands of fatherless children; pillage and confiscation have
> stripped them of the greater part of their belongings, their
> trades and crafts are broken down, their markets disorganized,
> and in wide regions there is nothing left from which a man may
> earn his bread. (16)

In England the Anglo-Armenian Association had many meetings under
the presidency of F.S. Stevenson, MP, and besought the British
Government to urge the Ottoman Porte to introduce reforms in the
administration of Turkish Armenia. An 'Armenian Relief Fund' was
organized in England in order to help the homeless and the poor in
Anatolia. The president of this Fund was the Duke of Argyll, and the
chairman F.S. Stevenson. The committee itself included such important persons as the Archbishop of York, Lord Edmond Fitzmaurice,
James Bryce, MP, John H. Kennaway, MP, and Charles E. Schwann, MP.

It must be noted here that Great Britain was the first among the
European States to intervene with the Ottoman Government to stop the
massacres. Russia, France and America joined her in an inquiry to
be made at the places where the massacres occurred. A special commission was organized with the following representatives: (17)

Tevfik Paşa, General of Brigade and Aide-de-camp,
Şefik Bey, President of one of the chambers of the Court of
    Cassation,
Celâleddin Bey, President of the Correctional section of the
    Court,
Necib Bey, Director of the Secretary-General's Office at the
    Ministry of Interior,
Ömer Bey, Director of the Savings Bank,
Mr H.S. Shipley, delegate of England,
Mr Prejewalsky, delegate of Russia,
Mr Vilbert, delegate of France,
Dr Miles Jewett, delegate of America. (18)

During the very time in which the Inquiry Commission had gone to
Erzurum and Bitlis to investigate the alleged outrages, massacres
were actually being carried out systematically in other parts of
Anatolia. On the demand of the commission the 'vali' of Bitlis
Tahsin Paşa was deprived of his post and provisionally replaced by
Ömer Bey at the end of January 1895. On their return to Istanbul
the European members of the commission presented to the Sublime
Porte the necessity of applying a programme for the reform of the
administration of Turkish Armenia. The Porte received the demands
of the European States, but the Sultan Abdülhamid was apparently not
yet satisfied with the blood already shed. In the following months
of 1895 the slaughter was continued in all the principal towns of
Turkey. These anti-Armenian outbreaks were crowned, in June 1896,
by the atrocities of Van, and in August 1896, by the massacre of
Istanbul. Thus in 1894-6 more than 300,000 Armenians perished
during the assaults organized by the Ottoman Porte.

At the end of the troubles, on 11 October 1896 the Porte issued
an Imperial decree which sanctioned some reforms respecting the
administration of Eastern Anatolia which were suggested by the
European commission. The reforming decree was composed of 16
chapters and 32 articles. (19) Although it was dated 'Cemaziyel
evvel' 1313H (21 October 1895), this date was faked in order to
cover the complicity of the Ottoman Government in the massacre. The
note in reply by the ambassadors of Great Britain, France and Russia
(Philip Curry for Great Britain, P. Cambon for France and Nelidov
for Russia) dated 24 October 1896 over a year later, supports my
conclusion. These were the main points of the reforms:

1. In Eastern Anatolia (or the 'provinces inhabited by
    Armenians') each 'vali' would be accompanied by a non-Muslim
    assistant (art. 1).
2. Likewise, the governors of 'sancaks' and 'kazas' would be
    accompanied by non-Muslim assistants (art. 2).
3. The governors of 'kazas' would be elected by the Ministry of
    the Interior from among the graduates of the civil school and
    appointed by Imperial decree. If there were not sufficient
    Christians graduated from the State school to assist the
    governors, then people experienced in Ottoman public life
    would be called to fill these posts (art. 3 and 4).
4. The number of non-Muslim officials in political administra-
    tion, police and 'gendarmerie' would be in accordance with
    the number of the Christian population and fixed by the
    permanent commission of control (art. 5).
5. The governors of 'nahiyes' would be elected among the
    majority and the assistant-governors from the minority (art.
    8).
6. Each 'vilâyet' was to be given a judicial inspectorate of
    about six members, half of whom would be Muslim and the
    others Christians (art. 19).
7. The number of Muslim and non-Muslim policemen in the
    'vilâyets' would be in proportion to the number of the Muslim
    and Christian inhabitants (art. 20).
8. The number of 'gendarmes' also would be in proportion to the
    number of the Muslim and Christian inhabitants (art. 22).
9. In order to improve the collection of taxes, the tax-

collectors should hand over the tax-bills to the 'muhtars' of villages and quarters. These, after collecting the taxes, would remit the money to the State coffers.
10. A dignified Muslim functionary was to be appointed and sent as High Commissioner by the Sublime Porte to the Eastern provinces to oversee the execution of the reforms. This Commissioner would be accompanied by a Christian assistant.

OFFICES AND OFFICIALS IN OTTOMAN PUBLIC ADMINISTRATION

During the nineteenth century the population of Anatolia, especially the Christians, suffered much through anarchy and oppression and from irresponsible officials. After the proclamation of 'Hatti hümayun' (18 February 1856) the Great Powers proposed plans of reform to the Sublime Porte, including the participation of Christians in the administrative apparatus. In 1860 the Grand Vizier Kibrisli Mehmed Paşa visited the provinces and personally listened to the complaints of the people and in October 1864 the new provincial regulation was promulgated in order to reform the administration of the Ottoman provinces. (20) By this enactment the Ottoman territories were divided into: (a) the 'vilâyet' (province); (b) the 'sancak' (subdivision of a 'vilâyet' = county); (c) the 'kaza' (administrative division next to 'sancak' = district); (d) 'nahiye' (subdivision of a 'kaza' = commune) and (e) 'kariye' (quarter or village).

The 'vilâyet' was to be governed by a 'vali', the 'sancak' by a 'mutasarrif', the 'kaza' by a 'kaymakam', the 'nahiye' by a 'müdür' and the 'kariye' by a 'muhtar'. The 'vali', who was appointed by the Sultan, possessed the executive power in all branches, apart from the military. Under his immediate authority were all the heads of the various administrative departments, and he was also in charge of the police of the province. Usually the 'vali' had an assistant ('muavin') who replaced him in case of absence or sickness. Where there was no 'muavin' available, the 'defterdar' (general director of the financial department of a province) assisted the governor general. The 'defterdar', although acting in co-operation with the 'vali', was immediately responsible to the Finance Minister at Istanbul. The 'mutasarrif', also appointed by the Sultan, carried out his office under the authority of the 'vali'. Apart from being the general administrator of a 'sancak', he was the head of its administrative council ('idare meclisi'), and of its boards of public works ('nafia') and of education ('maarif'). Other senior officials in a 'sancak', next below to the 'mutasarrif', were the deputy judge ('naib'), the chief accountant ('muhasebeci'), and the head of secretariat ('tahrirat müdürü'). The 'kaymakam' of a 'kaza', like the 'mutasarrif' was at the same time ex officio head of the administrative council and of the board of public works. His assistants were the deputy judge, the head of the financial department ('mal müdürü'), and the chief clerk ('tahrirat kâtibi'). The administrator of a 'nahiye', the 'müdür' was appointed by the general governor of the province, but he took instructions from the 'kaymakam' of his 'kaza'. He gathered the taxes, executed the sentences of the judicial court, and sometimes personally tried to pacify quarrels and disputes. The 'muhtar' (head man) of a 'kariye' was chosen by the inhabitants of his quarter or village and affirmed by the governor of his 'kaza'. He was assisted by a council whose members were mainly elders, for which reason it was called 'ihtiyar meclisi' (council of elders).

The Armenian officials in Ottoman public administration appear mostly in the 'kazas' and at the headquarters of the 'sancaks'. I shall therefore present here a general picture of the administrative apparatus at the centre of 'sancaks', and when there is a relevant department, in outlying 'kazas' also:

1. Political administration

(i) Administrative council
    (a) Ex officio member ('âza-i tabîiye')
        Governor general
        Deputy judge
        Head of financial department
        Mufti
        Armenian bishop
        Armenian Catholic bishop (or priest)
        Armenian Protestant pastor (sometimes)
        Greek metropolitan (if there was one)
In an outlying 'kaza' the ex officio members were: the governor, the deputy judge, the mufti, the head of the financial department and the chief secretary.
    (b) Elected members ('âza-i müntahab')
Usually two Christian and two Muslim members were elected.
In outlying 'kazas' also two Christians and two Muslims were generally elected to the Administrative council.
(ii) Municipality
    (a) Municipal council ('belediye meclisi')
        Mayor ('belediye reisi')
        Members (from 6 to 12)
In a normal 'kaza' the Municipal council had 5-10 members.
    (b) Municipal officials ('belediye memuru')
        Clerk ('kâtib')
        Cashier ('sandik emini')
        Engineer ('mühendis')
        Doctor ('tabib')
        Vaccinator ('aşi memuru')
        Midwife ('kabile')
        Inspector ('müfettiş')
        Inspector's assistant ('müfettiş muavini')
In a usual 'kaza' the Municipal officials were the same, but there were no inspectors.

2. Secretariat

(i) Chief secretariat (also for the Administrative council)
    Administrative council's clerk
    Documents' (archives) official ('evrak memuru')

   Chief clerk for drafting letter ('mûsevvid evvel')
   Second clerk for drafting letters ('mûsevvid sani')
   Chief copyist ('mûbeyyiz evvel')
   Second copyist
   Third copyist
   Assistants ('mûlâzim'), up to 8 in number
 (ii) Chamber of archives ('evrak odasi')
   Documents official
   An assistant
   Stationer ('kirtasiye memuru'). He was the official who pro-
    vided stationery, printed official forms and other papers
    to different governmental departments.
   Assistants (1-3)
(iii) State land registry ('defter hakanî idaresi')
   Chief official ('memur')
   Chief clerk
   Assistant clerk
   Title-deeds' clerk ('tapu kâtibi')
   Assistant to the clerk of title-deeds
 (iv) Secretariat to the financial department
   Chief official
   Chief clerk
   Assistant clerk
   Accountant
   Assistants (about 4)
   Cashier
 (v) Secretariat to the Court of first instance ('bidayet kalemi')
   Chief clerk
   Civil department's clerk (2)
   Criminal department's clerk (2)

3. Finance

 (i) Office of the controller of revenue and expenditure ('mal
   kalemi')
   Director ('mûdûr')
   Assistants (2)
   Cashier
   Lawyer for the treasury ('hazine dâva vekili')
 (ii) Taxation department ('vergi dairesi')
   Chief official
   Cashier
   Chief clerk
   Accountant
   Assistants (about 4)
 To the department of taxation was attached the Estimates'
committee ('heyet-i tahminiye'):
   Tax assessors, 2 ('vergi muhammini')
   Municipal tax assessors, 2 ('belediye muhammini')
(iii) Tax collection
  (a) Tax collecting board ('tahsilat komisyonu')
    The director ('reis'), who was the head of financial
     department

4 members:
1 from the Administrative council
1 from the Municipality
Chief tax collector ('ser tahsildar')
Clerk
(b) Tax collection committee ('tahsilat heyeti')
Chief official
Chief tax-collector
Clerk
Tax collectors, about 15. Some were pedestrian ('piyade
tahsildar') and the others mounted ('süvari tahsildar')
In the usual 'kazas' there were only tax collection committees
which included the same officials as in the central 'kazas' of
'sancaks'.
(iv) Chamber of commerce and agriculture ('Ticaret ve ziraat
odasi')
Director
Assistant
Members (about 6)
Clerk
In an outlying 'kaza' this chamber had a head, a clerk and about
4 members.
(v) Agricultural Bank branch ('Ziraat bankasi şubesi')
In 1868 the Ottomen Government established 'Credit offices' ('menafi
sandigi') which in 1888 were replaced by the branches of the Agri-
cultural Bank. Both the 'Credit offices' and the banks gave loans
to the farmers and agriculturists in order to improve agriculture.
In the present study under the heading 'Agricultural Bank branches'
must be understood also the 'Credit offices' for the period 1868-88.
(a) Cash account ('kasa idaresi')
Manager
Assistant
Clerk
In the cash account of the outlying 'kaza' there were: the
account's clerk and two assisting officials.
(b) The council
Head
Members (about 4)
The same officials were in the Agricultural Bank's council of the
outlying 'kaza'.
(vi) Branch of the Ottoman Bank ('Osmanli Bankasi şubesi')
Manager
Accountant
Branches of the Ottoman Bank were only very rarely to be found in
outlying 'kazas'.
(vii) Public Debt administration ('divan-i umumiye idaresi')
Chief official
Clerk
Cashier
Weighing-official ('kantarci')
Tax-collector
In a normal 'kaza' the Public debt had the same officials,
although not usually a special weigher.
(viii) Customs administration ('rüsumat nezareti')

       Administrator ('nazir')
       Accounts chief clerk
       Chief secretary
       Clerk
       Assistant clerk
  Offices of Custom administration are very rarely to be found in
outlying 'kazas'.
  (ix) 'Régie'
       Manager
       Accountant
       Store-keeper ('anbarci')
       Clerk
       Lawyer ('dâva vekili')
  In a usual 'kaza', the 'Régie' had the same officials, except for
a lawyer.

4. The court

In the central and outlying 'kazas' there were only courts of First
instance, whereas at the headquarters of the provinces courts of
appeal ('istinaf mahkemesi') were also established. In case of
difficulties, the disputes were transferred from an outlying 'kaza'
to the centre of the 'sancak' and if necessary, from there to the
court of appeal of the 'vilâyet'.
Court of First instance ('bidayet mahkemesi')
     (a) Civil department ('hukuk dairesi')
       Head (the deputy judge)
       Members (2)
       Assistant functionary ('mülâzim')
  In an outlying 'kaza' the Court had a head (the deputy judge),
2 members and 2 clerks.
     (b) Criminal department ('ceza dairesi')
       Head
       Members (2)
       Assistant functionary
       Public prosecutor ('müddei umumi')
     (c) Other court officials
       Executive officer ('icra memuru')
       'Juge d'instruction' ('müstantik')
       Notary ('mukavelât muharriri')
  The other court officials of a usual 'kaza', were: the 'juge
d'instruction', the public prosecutor, and the notary.
     (d) Commercial court
       Head
       Members (4)

5. Technical departments
  (i) Public works
     (a) Public work's board ('nafia komisyonu')
       Head (the governor)
       Members: Manager of the Agricultural Bank
                Member from the Administrative council

                    Member from the Municipality
                    Member from the Chamber of commerce
                    Registrar of births or census officer ('nüfus
                       memuru')
                    Public works engineer
                    Clerk
   In a normal 'kaza' the Public works' board had a head (who was
the 'kaymakam') and 4 members: one from the Administrative council,
the accounts' clerk of the Agricultural Bank branch, the registrar
of births, and one from the Chief secretariat or any other member.
      (b) Technicians ('memurin-i fenniye')
          Engineer
          Two foremen ('kondoktor')
(ii) Post and telegraph ('posta ve telgraf idaresi')
     Postmaster ('posta müdürü')
     Telegraphic superintendents, 2 ('muhabere memuru')
     Linesman foreman ('hat çavuşu')
     Clerk
     Postmen, 2 ('müvezzi')
     Postal messenger ('posta şakirdi')
   In the postal and telegraphic service of a usual 'kaza' there
were: the postmaster, a telegraph superintendent, and a clerk.

6. Public health service

 (i) Municipality's service (see under Municipality)
(ii) Public health board ('heyet-i sihhiye')
     Doctor
     Chemist
     Vaccinator
     Midwife
     Veterinary surgeon ('baytar')

7. Education

 (i) Educational board ('maarif komisyonu')
     First director
     Second director
     Members (about 8)
     Clerks (1 or 2)
   In an outlying 'kaza' the Educational board had a head and about
5 members.
(ii) School of handicrafts ('sanayi mektebi')
     Director
     Teacher (of general subjects)
     Teachers of joinery, blacksmiths' art, shoemaking, etc.

8. Forest administration ('orman idaresi')

     Superintendent of mounted foresters ('orman süvari memuru')
     Tithe officials, 3 ('ondalik memuru')

Forest-guards, 3 ('korucu')
In an outlying 'kaza' normally there was only one official for forest tithes.

Chapter 1

THE ARMENIANS OF DIYARBAKIR

HISTORICAL SURVEY

Diyarbakir (the ancient Amida) lies on the western bank of the
Tigris and includes the larger part of the regions of Dzophq and
Aghzniq (Arzanena, Arzan) of ancient Armenia. In 94-93 BC Dzophq
was joined to Greater Armenia by the King Tigran II. Later it was
occupied by the Romans and Byzantines, and in AD 536 the Emperor
Justinian made it a Byzantine province calling it Fourth Armenia.
    In 19H/640, during the caliphate of Umar ibn al-Khattâb and under
the commandment of Iyâd ibn Ghannâm al-Nahrî the Arabs conquered
Diyarbakir. In 958 the Byzantines succeeded in regaining it, but in
1070 the Seljuk Alp Arslan, and in 1093 the Melik of Syria Tâdj al-
Dawla Tutush took possession of it. In 1183 Salâh al-Dîn b. Ayyûb
occupied Diyarbakir, ceding it to his ally the Artuqid Nûr al-Dîn
Muhammad. In the thirteenth century it fell to the Mongol domination, but after 1335 it was governed by Turkomans.
    In 908H/1502-3 Diyarbakir was vanquished by the Safawî Shâh
Ismâ'îl who appointed the Qara Hasan Ustâclu-oglu as 'vali'. The
Persian control, however, did not last long. The Ottomans taking
advantage of the insubordination of the inhabitants, during 921-3H/
1515-17 under the leadership of the vizier of the Sultan Selîm I
(1512-20), Biyikli Mehmed Paşa, finally brought Diyarbakir under the
direct government of the Sublime Porte.

ADMINISTRATIVE STRUCTURE

The 'vilâyet' of Diyarbakir was first created in 1867. It had four
administrative subdivisions: Diyarbakir, Ergani, Mardin, and
Malatya. In 1297H/1879-80 one part of Diyarbakir was made the
'vilâyet' of Elâzig which included Malatya. The remaining three
'sancaks', were divided into fourteen 'kazas' as follows.
The 'kazas' of the 'sancak' of Diyarbakir (Diyârbakir):
    Diyarbakir
    Siverek
    Derik
    Lice

Beşiri
Silvan with its centre at Miyafarkin (now called Silvan).
    Miyafarkin (previously named Maipheracta, Npherkert and
    Martyropolis), is the ancient Tigranocerta, which was built by
    the Armenian King Tigran II about 80 BC. It was a notable
    centre for trade and transport. (1)
'Sancak' of Ergani (formerly called Argana Ma'den, Argana and some-
times Osmaniye), had three 'kazas':
    Ergani
    Palu
    Çermik which included the 'nahiye' of Cüngüş.
The 'kazas' of the 'sancak' of Mardin:
    Mardin
    Nüsaybin
    Cizre
    Midyat
    Avine

POPULATION

In the second half of the nineteenth century the total population of
the 'vilâyet' of Diyarbakir, according to Cuinet (2) was 471,462,
Muslims, Christians and others. The non-Muslim population was as
follows:
    Armenians
        Apostolic (3)   57,890
        Catholic   10,170
        Protestant   11,069
                                            79,129
    Greeks
        Orthodox   9,250
        Catholic   190
                                             9,440
    Chaldeans   16,420
    Syrians (mostly Orthodox)   27,544
    Latins   16
    Jews   1,269
                                          ―――――――
                    Total   133,818
Something which becomes apparent in considering the population of
Ottoman Empire is the great difference between the figures quoted by
Turkish and Armenian publications. In Turkish sources the number of
Armenians in Turkey has been underestimated in order to minimize the
importance of the Armenian Question and to divert the attention of
Europeans. Cuinet, who has used mainly Turkish sources, gives the
number of Armenians in Diyarbakir as 79,129. (4) Published at the
same time, an Armenian booklet (5) records that 355,000 people, of
whom 120,000 were Armenians, were living in Diyarbakir. Also the
almanac of Theodik informs us that the Armenians in Diyarbakir
before the First World War were 124,000. (6) It will be seen that
while the Turks have reduced the number of Armenians, some Armenians
have exaggerated their statistics. Therefore we can only approximate the total of the Armenians in Diyarbakir, by taking the mean

between the number given by Cuinet and the figures by the Armenian
sources mentioned above. Thus we have a total estimated population
of Armenians in the region of 100,000.

It is worthy of note that the statistical analysis of the racial
elements in Eastern Anatolia, drawn up in 1912 by the Armenian
Patriarchate of Istanbul, attests to the fact that the Armenians of
Diyarbakir numbered 105,000, which confirms our estimate. The
following are the figures taken from this statistical analysis concerning Diyarbakir: (7)

Armenians	105,000
Nestorians, Jacobites and Chaldeans	60,000
Turks	45,000
Kurds	50,000
Kizilbash (Shiites)	27,000
Yezidis	4,000
Total	291,000

J. Lepsius (8) also gives the same figure of 105,000 for the number
of Armenians in the province of Diyarbakir, but 63,000 for the
Turks, thus:

Armenians	105,000
Syrians (Nestorians and Chaldeans)	60,000
Greeks	1,000
Kurds	200,000
Turks	63,000
Kizilbash	27,000
Circassians	10,000
Yezidis	4,000
Jews	1,500
Total	471,500

It appears from these statistics that the Armenians living in
Diyarbakir were more numerous than the Turks.

TRADES AND PROFESSIONS OF ARMENIANS

In the second half of the nineteenth century, in the province of
Diyarbakir, especially at the towns of Diyarbakir and Mardin, trade
and industry were in a flourishing state. The main productions were
silk and cotton textiles, articles of copper and earthenware, and
morocco leather. The Armenians took an active part in local trade
and manufacturing as skilled craftsmen, merchants and artisans.
Martiros Attarian was a famous manufacturer of Turkish linen,
Tchavrashian was a well-known tailor, while architecture was
practised almost entirely by Armenians. We have an interesting eye-
witness account of a traveller on the business of the Armenians of
Diyarbakir as early as the seventeenth century. The scribe Siméon
from Lwow who visited there in 1612 describes the situation of
Armenians in the town of Diyarbakir itself as the following:

There are 1,000 Armenian houses and all of them are wealthy,
luxurious and glorious. And whatever business and riches exist,

they possess: the mint, the customs, caravanserais and the rest.
Also the cooks, restaurant proprietors, bakers, grocers and the
butchers, are all Armenian.   And, when it is Sunday or a holiday,
and the Armenians do not open their shops and do not work, you
think [the town] is empty and desolated. (9)
The 'kaza' of Palu in the 'sancak' of Ergani which was densely
populated by Armenians, was also a centre of commerce and crafts.
Nathanian, having visited Palu in 1878-9, attests the following concerning the activity of Armenians there:

> Merchandise for twelve thousand Turkish pounds per annum is
> imported into Palu. Most of the importers and exporters of the
> articles are Armenian.   There is a market of medium size where
> there are about three hundred shops, two caravanserais built of
> brick and stone, and four bakeries. Most of the craftsmen and
> traders of this market are Armenian. (10)

Members of the Armenian community were also occupied in different
professions, especially in law, medicine and pharmacy, of whom the
names of Boghos Efendi Der-Gabrielian (lawyer, fl.c. 1890), Karapet
(Garabed) Efendi Dabaghian (lawyer, fl.c. 1890), Kirakos Efendi
Enovchian (lawyer, fl.c. 1890), Dr Tchibukdjian (municipal doctor,
fl.c. 1892), Dr Artin Helvadjian (army physician, fl.c. 1890), Yakob
Hekimian (municipal chemist, fl.c. 1892), and Artin Aghkekian (municipal chemist, fl.c. 1892) can be mentioned.

CENTRES OF ARMENIAN PARTICIPATION

Armenians, living all over the 'vilâyet' of Diyarbakir, participated
in the public life of the whole province. Localities where they
particularly contributed were the centres of the 'sancaks', and the
'kazas' of Siverek, Lice and Derik in the 'sancak' of Diyarbakir
itself; Palu and Çermik at Ergani, and Midyat, Avine and Cizre in
Mardin.
     The city of Diyarbakir was inhabited by 10,260 Armenians who
constituted one-third of the whole population of 35,000. As the
offices of the central government of the province were situated in
the town, Armenians took an important part in the local life, con-
tributing much to the political administration, justice, finance,
technical affairs, education and public health.

MAIN FIELDS OF ARMENIAN PARTICIPATION

The Armenians in the centres of the province of Diyarbakir served in
most of the governmental departments. In the 'kazas' they regularly
took part in political administration, justice, finance and
mechanics. These posts were, hence, the main fields of Armenian
influence.
     In the administrative councils of the 'sancaks' and 'kazas', the
Armenians were usually represented by two elected members. They had
one or two ex officio members as well, the latter being the
spiritual heads of the Apostolic and Catholic communities or sometimes of the Protestant, where they were relatively numerous. There
was also a lay member ex officio, if he held a high position in the

government such as deputy-governor, controller of revenue and
expenditure or chief secretary. In the 'nahiyes' the assistants to
the administrators were often Armenian, and from one to three were
members or clerks to the local councils. Many from the Armenian
community were appointed to the municipal councils. Here up to five
elected members, cashiers and clerks were Armenian, as sometimes was
the mayor. This department was the branch in which the Armenians
were occasionally in the majority. In the judicature the Armenians
were included in the courts of first instance, appeal and of commerce. In the commercial courts the Armenian and Greek officials
were more numerous than Turks, because, we presume, the trade was
for the most part in their hands. Another sphere of Armenian influence was the committee for public prosecution. Government
lawyers were found especially in the central parts of the province.
In mechanical affairs Armenians served chiefly as engineers and
foremen; in the postal and telegraphic service as operators, especially in the foreign language sections; in public works, and on
military transport boards. With regard to finance, Armenians played
an important role in the public debt administration, the state
tobacco monopoly, at the branches of the Ottoman and Agricultural
Banks, and tax committees, though in these they did not hold a
dominant position.

OTHER FIELDS OF ARMENIAN PARTICIPATION

Facets of Armenian participation other than the above mentioned,
were those of the departments of the secretariat, public health,
education, agriculture and police. The Armenian officials worked as
clerks to the administrative councils, judicial courts, investigation committees for title-deeds ('tedkik-i senedat komisyonu') and
the board of records ('evrak komisyonu'). They were also employed
as clerks and translators in the postal and telegraphic service and
were always included on the chief secretarial commissions ('tahrirat
komisyonu').

    There was a preponderance of Armenian municipal doctors and
chemists, and next to them came Greek medical officials. In
Diyarbakir city and in the centres of the 'sancaks' of Mardin and
Ergani, Armenians sat on the educational councils and committees.
They also taught Armenian and European languages in the schools, as
well as crafts, particularly carpet making. In agriculture,
Armenians were appointed members, both to the branches of the Agricultural Bank and to the agricultural boards and committees. They
also worked on the land inspection and land registry commissions.
The police force accepted a very small number of Armenians as
policemen and assistant superintendents of police. Where there were
from five to nine Turkish policemen in a station there would be only
one or two Armenians.

COMPARATIVE NOTE: GREEK AND SYRIAN PARTICIPATION

The public life of the province was, on the whole, directed by Turks
and Armenians, these latter being in the majority among the

Christian population. However, to a certain extent Greeks and
Syrians also made some contribution. Greek officials, mainly in the
centre of the 'sancaks' of Diyarbakir, Mardin and Ergani, participated in judicature, finance, political administration, technical
affairs and public health. It has to be noticed that in the army
Greek doctors, surgeons and chemists were more numerous than the
Armenians.

Syrian Christian officials were to be found throughout the province and particularly at Mardin, but there were not as many Syrians
as Greeks. They were usually to be found in the administrative and
municipal councils, but a few held posts also in judicature and
finance.

A GENERAL VIEW OF ARMENIAN PARTICIPATION IN DIYARBAKIR

The Armenians between 1860 and 1908 served the province of
Diyarbakir in many ways. They participated in almost all aspects of
governmental affairs, acting in different posts in the political
administration, justice, mechanical works, finance, public health,
education and the secretariat. As Christians they were exempt from
the fighting forces and from the departments connected with Islamic
life, the Muslim religious court ('mahkeme-i şer'i şerif') and Pious
Foundation ('vakif'). It is worthy of note that they were barred
from the registry of births ('nüfüs dairesi'), and very few were
accepted in the police department. The Armenians in the administration of public life were mostly subordinate officials, very
rarely being given high position. They were usually appointed or
elected as members of councils, departments and committees, as
cashiers and clerks. Frequently an Armenian held the office of
treasurer in various departments, not for the reason that they were
wealthier than the Muslim population but probably because the Turks
relied on them in financial affairs. The functions of high rank
sometimes granted to Armenians were administrative and judicial. We
occasionally find Armenians as mayors, assistant administrators of
'nahiyes', or general district attorneys. They were also specialist
and technical officials such as municipal doctors, chemists and
public works' engineers.

Viewing the public life of Diyarbakir as a whole within this
period, we notice that generally the Armenians were in a minority
compared with the Muslims.

SOME NOTABLE ARMENIANS IN THE PUBLIC LIFE OF DIYARBAKIR

AMASIAN Efendi. About 1892 he was the head of telegraphic service
in Diyarbakir.
ARMENAK Efendi. In 1903 he was an assistant to the deputy-governor
of the 'kaza' of Palu.
ARPIARIAN, Philippos (fl. in the second half of the nineteenth century). Originally from Harput, he was a manager of the Agricultural
Bank in Diyarbakir.
DER-MARTIROSIAN (Papazian), Meguerditch (1792-1883). Born in the
village of Abuçeh of Kemaliye, he studied medicine under his uncle

Dr Boghos and an Italian physician.   In 1826 he obtained permission
from Istanbul to practise medicine, and thereafter was employed in
the Turkish army.   He followed the army in Baghdad, Bassora,
Diyarbakir, Van and Erzurum.   He retired in 1872 and returned to his
native village.

DJENAZIAN, Mattheos Efendi.   He was cashier of public finance
administration at Diyarbakir (?-1898).   Before him his brother
Alexandr Efendi held the same post, who, in his return had succeeded
his father Araqel (fl.c. 1860).

DJERRAHIAN, Tigran (fl.c. 1900).   He was a member of public prosecution board in Diyarbakir.

HEKIMIAN, Yakob (fl. in the second half of the nineteenth century).
A chemist who worked for the government in Diyarbakir.

HELVADJIAN, Dr Artin (fl. in the second half of the nineteenth century).   A doctor who worked for the government in Diyarbakir.

ILVANIAN, Tigran (?-1915).   About 1900 he was the provincial translator of Diyarbakir, and at the same time a teacher in the government secondary school.

KAZAZIAN, Yovseph Efendi (fl.c. 1880).   A wealthy and influential
Armenian Catholic who was a member of the administrative council of
Diyarbakir.

KHANDENIAN, Karapet (fl.c. 1900).   He was a member of the court of
first instance (in the criminal section) of Diyarbakir.

KIRISHDJIAN, Tigran Efendi.   From 1905 to 1908 he was the assistant
to the governor of the 'kaza' of Palu.

MARKOSIAN, Pargew (Barkev) Efendi.   From 1903 to 1906 he was the
engineer and inspector of forests and mining in the 'sancak' of
Ergani.

MINASIAN, Yaruthiwn (fl. in the second half of the nineteenth century).   He was the head of the post office in Diyarbakir.

MINASIAN, Yovhannes Efendi.   He was a member of the administrative
council of Diyarbakir from 1906 to 1908.

NAKKASHIAN, Karapet-Tigran Efendi (1864-?).   Born in Diyarbakir, he
attended the local Armenian primary school, and then taught himself
four European languages and in 1885 became an official in the telegraphic services.   Later, in Istanbul, he was appointed chief of the
Pera (Beyoglu) office;   in 1909 assistant director, and in 1912 was
made director of telegraph office.

NATIK, Karapet (fl. in the second half of the nineteenth century).
A lawyer who worked for the government in Diyabakir.

NISHAN Efendi.   From 1903 to 1908 he was assistant to the deputy-
governor of Maden.

SHIRIKDJIAN, Missak.   He was a member of the municipal council of
Diyarbakir about 1900.

SHISHMANIAN, Sahak Efendi.   He was the editor of the government
official newspaper 'Diyârbakir' about 1880.

TCHELEBIAN, Rizqallah (fl. in the second half of the nineteenth century).   He was a judge of the court of appeal in Diyarbakir.

TCHIRADJIAN, Khosrov (fl.c. 1900).   Educated in the Euphrates
College of Harput, he was a clerk to the public prosecution board of
Diyarbakir.

TEMOYAN, Boghos (fl. in the second half of the nineteenth century).
He was a member of the municipal council in Diyarbakir.

TIGRANIAN, Khatchadur (?-1915).   A banker who was a member of the

administrative council of Diyarbakir.
ZORIAN, Kevork (fl.c. 1892). He was an official in the postal and telegraphic service in Diyarbakir, working in the section of foreign languages.

Chapter 2

THE ARMENIANS OF BITLIS

HISTORICAL SURVEY

Bitlis (Arm. Baghêsh, whence Arb. Badlîs or Bidlîs, Ott.Turk,
Bitlîs) included the larger part of the regions of Taron-Turuberan
and Aghzniq of ancient Armenia.

In 20H/640-1 the Arabs subdued the districts of Bitlis, Muş and
Siirt, but in 885 the Armenians threw off the yoke of Arab domination under the leadership of the princes of the Bagratid (Bagratuni)
dynasty and established a kingdom which lasted until 1054. In the
eleventh century the Seljuks, and in the fourteenth the Mongols, conquered Bitlis and its surroundings. Shortly afterwards came the
Ottoman Turks, and as the aggressive Kurdish tribes, probably
immigrating from Persia, had become a large element in Bitlis, Muş
and Van, it was the Kurdish chief who ruled under the suzerainty of
the Ottomans. In 1263H/1846 the Ottomans broke the power of the
Kurds and brought these territories under the direct subordination
of their regular government.

ADMINISTRATIVE STRUCTURE

Bitlis and Muş were formerly included in the 'eyalet' (government-
general) of Erzurum. In 1292H/1875 they were detached and made a
separate 'vilâyet'. The 'sancak' of Siirt which had formed a part
of the province of Diyarbakir, in 1301H/1883-4 was joined to the
'vilâyet' of Bitlis.

The province of Bitlis contained four 'sancaks' which were
divided into nineteen 'kazas'. The provincial governor's residence
was in the city of Bitlis. In the towns of Muş, Siirt and Genç were
found the residences of the 'sancak'-governors, and each of the
other 'kazas' was administrated by a sub-governor. The administrative division and subdivisions of the province of Bitlis was as
follows.
The 'kazas' of the 'sancak' of Bitlis:
   Bitlis
   Ahlat
   Hizan
   Mutki

The 'kazas' of the 'sancak' of Muş:
  Muş
  Bulanik
  Malazgirt
  Varto
  Sasun (Kabilcevaz)
The 'kazas' of the 'sancak' of Siirt:
  Siirt
  Ridvan
  Şirvan
  Eruh
  Kurtalan (Garzan)
  Pervari
  Kozluk (Hazzo)
The 'kazas' of the 'sancak' of Bingöl: (1)
  Genç
  Bingöl (Çapakçur)
  Kulp

POPULATION

The population of the province of Bitlis in the second half of the
nineteenth century was estimated by Cuinet as 398,625, and he
divided it as follows:
  Armenians
        Apostolic   125,600
        Catholic   3,840
        Protestant   1,950
                                    131,390
  Greek Orthodox   210
  Chaldeans   2,600
  Syrian Orthodox (2)   6,190
  Copts   372
  Muslims   254,000
  Yezidis   3,863
                                    _____
                Total   398,625

These statistics are based mainly on Turkish sources. The Armenian
authors give different figures for the population of the province of
Bitlis. Ormanian, (3) followed by Lepsius, (4) estimates the number
of Armenians as 196,000; the Armenian Patriarchate at Istanbul as
180,000; (5) the Theodik's almanac as 198,000, (6) and M.A. as
308,000. (7) I prefer to accept the figures of the Armenian
Patriarchate as giving the most probable approximate total of the
Armenians who lived in Bitlis, as this presents the mean of two
extreme estimates.
     The statistical analysis produced by the Armenian Patriarchate
for the racial elements in the province, is:

Armenians	180,000
Nestorians, Syrians and Chaldeans	15,000
Turks	40,000
Kurds	77,000
Circassians	10,000
Kizilbash	8,000
Yezidis	5,000
Zaza, Timbali and Çarikli (8)	47,000
Total	382,000

According to this table it can be seen that from a racial point of view the Armenians were the largest community in Bitlis.

TRADES AND PROFESSIONS OF ARMENIANS

Bitlis was a centre of commerce being on the intersection of the Tiflis-Trebizond route, and connected southward with routes to Syria and Mosul. The Armenians in some parts of the province were occupied in agriculture and cattle breeding, but their main employment was in trade and crafts. In the manufacture of carpets, cloth and domestic utensils the Armenians competed with Kurds and Turks, but the rest of commerce and handicrafts was largely in their hands. They were engaged in many trades; in the goldsmith's art, sewing, painting, building, blacksmith's craft, farriery, pottery, woodwork, shoe making and general trade. A. Dô, an Armenian writer who visited Bitlis in 1909, records the occupation of Armenians thus:
> The Armenians of Bitlis are skilled and have natural ability. They show a special flare for trade. In this district the commerce is for the major part in their hands, although disturbances and massacres have repeatedly come to disrupt the activities and production of this resilient people. (9)

The same author states that of 800 shops in the town of Muş, 500 belonged to Armenians: 200 of these shop keepers dealt in retail commerce and the remainder were craftsmen. Lynch, who visited Muş in 1893, gave this eye-witness account concerning the occupation of Armenians there:
> The Armenian minority are artisans, smiths, makers of everything that is manufactured in Mush. They are carpenters, plasterers, builders. All keepers of booths which we passed in the bazaar plainly belonged to this race. (10)

In Siirt the Armenians were also engaged in trade and handicrafts.

CENTRES OF ARMENIAN PARTICIPATION

The Armenians in the province of Bitlis, as in other parts of the Ottoman Empire, were mostly concentrated in the towns. According to the statistics of Cuinet nearly one-third of the whole Armenian population of the province lived in the towns of Bitlis, Muş, Siirt and Genç. This situation was the controlling factor in the participation of the Armenian community in public life. Although Armenians of Bitlis served the government throughout the province, the special spheres of Armenian influence were the towns of Bitlis, Muş, Siirt and Genç, where the headquarters of the 'sancaks' were situated. Other centres where there was a marked Armenian contribution to public life, were Ahlat in Bitlis, the 'kazas' of Bulanik and Malazgirt in Muş, Eruh in Siirt, and Kulp in the 'sancak' of Bingöl (Genç).

It is significant that in the 'kaza' of Sasun (Kabilcevaz) where the Armenian population countered persecution with a spirit of independence, they were engaged little in public administration, whereas in Saimbeyli (Haçin) in the province of Adana, and in Süleymanli (Zeytun) in the province of Aleppo, where the Armenians were also remarkably independent, their officials held a dominant position in all departments of local government. What was the reason for this difference? It could have been because in Saimbeyli and Süleymanli, both districts of Little Armenia, there was European influence, and even intervention in the case of Süleymanli, and also possibly because the Turks felt safer about Cilicia than Muş, which was near to the Russian border.

MAIN FIELDS OF ARMENIAN PARTICIPATION

The main fields of public life of Bitlis into which the Armenians entered were government politics, justice, finance and the secretariat. At the seats of the 'sancaks', Armenians were to be found in nearly every department; more were employed in some departments than in others, but the principle governing the proportions is not clear. Perhaps there was some nepotism; it may have been pure chance, but more probably, the qualifications required for certain positions made the Armenians particularly suitable. In the 'kazas' where the offices were comparatively limited they contributed constantly to the public administration. Two Armenians were usually elected to the administrative councils at the centres of 'sancaks'. Besides these the spiritual heads of the Apostolic communities were ex officio members, as were also the assistant governors who after 1896 were normally Armenian. In the councils of 'kazas' we find one or, more often, two Armenians who were at all times elected members. Two or three Armenians were also elected to the municipal councils at the central headquarters of the 'sancaks' of Bitlis, Muş and Siirt. There were fewer in the municipalities of the other parts of the province, except in the 'kazas' of Bulanik and Varto in the 'sancak' of Muş where there was a permanent and quite strong Armenian influence.

In the judicature there were about as many Armenian judges as Turkish. The courts in the 'kazas' had one Armenian member. At the centres of the 'sancaks' there were usually two Armenians in the courts of first instance, and of appeal, one for the civil division, and the other for the criminal division, and either two or three in the commercial courts. For the 'sancak'-governments in the towns of Bitlis, Muş and Siirt, Armenians also acted as members of the boards of public prosecution, executive officers, assistants to the 'juges d'instruction' and process-servers ('mübaşir'). In the financial spheres of Bitlis Armenians were much occupied in manufacture and

commerce.   Apart from that, from one to three of them were employed
on the board of tax collection;   one or two in the branches of the
Ottoman and Agricultural Banks;   one or two in the state tobacco
industry;   one in the public debt administration, and one as controller in the revenue.   This was the situation in the 'sancaks' of
Bitlis and Muş, but in Siirt and Bingöl the Armenian officials were
included only on the committee of tax collection, in the control of
revenue and in the administration of public debt.

The main function of the Armenians in the public administration
of the province was the secretariat.   They were clerks to the administrative councils, to banks, to land registries, to registrars
of birth, to investigation committees for title-deeds, and to
military transport committees.

OTHER FIELDS OF ARMENIAN PARTICIPATION

We also find Armenians engaged in the technical services, police,
education and public health.   In the centres of the 'sancaks'
Armenians worked in the civil engineering departments as engineers
and foremen in the public works, in the press and in the postal and
telegraphic services.   In the junior positions of the police forces
and on the education committees of each of the 'kazas' were to be
found one or two Armenians, and a few Armenian doctors were also
attached to the municipal councils.

COMPARATIVE NOTE: GREEK, SYRIAN AND KURDISH OFFICIALS

As there were only 210 Greeks living in the entire province, these
being concentrated in the 'kaza' of Ahlat in the 'sancak' of Bitlis,
very few of them were occupied in public affairs.   Some however
worked in the police, in political administration, in public health
and in the post offices.   It is significant that they were appointed
as superintendents of police, while the far more numerous Armenians
were never selected.   The Ottomans pursued this policy of appearing
to patronize Christians while at the same time ensuring that the
large Armenian community could not use this organization to exert
their own independence.

The Syrian population, which was larger than the Greek, was concentrated in Bitlis and Siirt.   So in these 'sancaks' especially
several Syrian officials worked in public life, notably in the
administrative councils.

The Kurds, who were more numerous than both the Greeks and
Syrians, also took part in local government.   Some of them were
members of administrative councils and judicial courts, some were
policemen, some tax collectors, and others were assistants to the
administrators of 'nahiyes'.

A GENERAL VIEW OF ARMENIAN PARTICIPATION IN BITLIS

Looking at the participation of the Armenians in the public life of
Bitlis as a whole, we can conclude that their particular

contribution was in political administration, judicature and finance.   While there were not sufficient Armenians in Bingöl (Genç) to have any great effect on that 'sancak', they had a large share in the public administration of the 'sancaks' of Bitlis, Muş and Siirt.

From 1896 onwards, as a result of intervention by European Powers, the part which Armenians played in the government of the province of Bitlis increased and became more established.   In political administration Armenians were given the posts of assistants to the governors of the 'vilâyet', and of the 'sancaks' and 'kazas'.   They were usually employed as cashiers, clerks or members of the administrative, judicial, and financial councils and committees.   We do not find them as heads of departments or chairmen of councils or committees.   Therefore, even when the Armenians were equal in number to the Turkish officials in any department, they did not have a decisive influence since the director was Turkish.

SOME NOTABLE ARMENIANS IN THE PUBLIC LIFE OF BITLIS

ALIXANIAN, Nazareth.   He was the assistant to the governor of the 'sancak' of Muş from 1903 to 1904.
ALIXANIAN, Nishan.   He was the assistant to the governor of the 'sancak' of Muş from 1905 to 1906.
BEKMEZIAN, Anton Efendi (fl.c. 1898).   From about 1898 to 1901 he was the assistant to the 'vali' of Bitlis, and at the same time he acted as an ex officio member of the local administrative council, and as the head of the tax revenue board.
DER-NERSESIAN, Smbat.   He was the assistant to the 'vali' of Bitlis from 1902 to 1903.
HAMAMDJIAN, Yakob Efendi.   From about 1899 to 1903 he was the assistant to the governor of the 'sancak' of Muş.   (Is this the same person as the Yakob Efendi who at that time is mentioned as the assistant of the deputy-governor of the 'kaza' of Genç?)
SARKIS (Sargis) Efendi.   He was the assistant to the deputy-governor of the 'kaza' of Şirvan in the 'sancak' of Siirt.

Chapter 3

THE ARMENIANS OF VAN

HISTORICAL SURVEY

Van (Urartian Biaina-Buana whence Van in Arm., Arb. Wân, Ott.Turk.
Vân) covered the regions of Vaspurakan, Mokq and Kordjêq of ancient
Armenia. It was a centre of culture, in and around which the
civilization of the Urartians flourished.

The first Arab invasion of Armenia, about 19H/640, passed through
Artaz (Vaspurakan), without establishing an Arab settlement in the
country. From the middle of the eighth century, the Armenian
satrappy of Ardzruni ruled Vaspurakan, being dependent on the
Bagratid (Bagratuni) kingdom, under the suzerainty of the Arabs. In
the ninth century Arab colonies were founded in Vaspurakan at
Malazgirt, and on the north-eastern shores of Lake Van, at Bargiri
and Amiuk.

In 1021 Seneqerim, the vassal king of Vaspurakan, being attacked
from all quarters, ceded his territories to the Emperor Basil II in
exchange for Sivas, where he settled, bringing with him thousands of
families. As a result of the battle of Malazgirt against the
Seljuks, on 26 August 1071 the Byzantines lost completely their control of Armenia. After this the number of Kurds in Van began to in-
crease rapidly, probably immigrating from Persia. Among the Kurdish
tribes the Hakkâri who were the most powerful, occupied the regions to
the south and to the east of Van, renamed them Hakkâri and seized
the control of the local government. On 5 September 1387 the Mongol
Emperor Tîmûr Lenk captured Van, killed some 3,000 of the inhabitants and appointed Izz al-Dîn as governor of the province of
Kurdistan.

In August 1548 the Ottoman Sultan Süleyman I Qânûnî the
Magnificent conquered Van and made the 'defterdar' (minister of
finance) Çerkez Iskender Paşa governor. Between the sixteenth and
nineteenth centuries, the Kurdish tribes, led by the Hakkâris, continued to govern Van and Hakkâri, under the Ottoman overlordship.
In 1263H/1847 the Ottomans, alarmed by the Kurds' increasing power,
brought Kurdistan under their direct control.

In April 1915 when the Young Turks began to massacre and deport
the Armenian inhabitants of Anatolia, the Armenians of Van resisted
and defended themselves. Since they could not elicit support from

outside, the majority fled to Russia, Armenia, Iran and Mesopotamia.

ADMINISTRATIVE STRUCTURE

Van once formed a part of the 'vilâyet' of Erzurum, but in 1875 it
was detached and constituted a separate province. In 1888 Hakkâri
was added to it as a 'sancak'. Consequently the province of Van had
two 'sancaks' and nineteen 'kazas'.
The 'kazas' of the 'sancak' of Van:
  Van
  Karçgan – this region is now erased from the map of Turkey. It
     bordered Bitlis on the west, Gevaş on the east, the Lake Van
     on the north, and Mükus on the south. Apparently it is
     absorbed in the 'kazas' of Tatvan and Hizan in the province of
     Bitlis.
  Şatak
  Gevaş
  Adilcevaz
  Erciş
  Muradiye (Bargiri)
  Mükus
The 'kazas' of the 'sancak' of Hakkâri:
  Hakkâri (Çölemerik)
  Başkale (Elbak)
  Yüksekova (Gevar)
  Şemdinli (Şemdinan)
  Özalp (Mahmudi)
  Norduz
  Çal
  Hoşap (Mamuret ül-Hamid)
  Beytüşşebap
  Oramor
  Imadiye (now belongs to the Republic of Iraq)
The 'vali' and the principal officials resided at the Gardens (Arm.
Aygestan), in the town of Van, and the 'sancak'-governor of Hakkâri
at Çölemerik. Each of the other 'kazas' of the province was ad-
ministrated by a sub-governor.

POPULATION

In 1862 the British Consul R.A.O. Dalyell reported that the total
population of the province of Van was 418,700, of whom 209,100 were
Christian, and 209,600 Muslim, as follows:
  'Sancak' of Van: (1)
      Christians   90,100
      Muslims   95,100
                                        185,200

  'Sancak' of Hakkâri:
      Christians   119,000
      Muslims (mostly Kurds) 114,500
                                        233,500

                      Total   418,700

In 1890 Cuinet (2) reckoned the total population of the province as
430,000, of whom 178,000 were Christian and 252,000 non-Christian,
as follows:

Armenians

Apostolic	79,000	
Catholic	708	
Protestant	290	
		79,998

Syrians

Nestorians	40,000	
Orthodox	52,000	
		92,000
Chaldeans		6,000
Latins		2
Kurds		210,000
Turks		30,500
Circassians		500
Jews		5,000
Yezidis		5,400
Gipsies		600
Total		430,000

The statistics used by Cuinet were distorted in favour of the Turks.
The reason for this is quite clear. In Van and Erzurum the
Armenians, being more numerous than any of the other races, desired
some independence. By publishing figures which showed a numerical
inferiority of the Armenians, the Turks rejected their claim. To
give an idea of this distortion, it is sufficient to mention that
while the Consuls Dalyell and J.G. Taylor, (3) followed by Lynch,
record the Armenian population of the 'kaza' of Van as 42,000 and
the Muslim as 17,000, Cuinet's figures are 13,500 for the Armenians,
and 21,500 for the Muslims.

M.A., (4) contemporary with Cuinet, assessed the number of
Armenians in the province of Van as 194,000, and even as late as the
early years of the twentieth century Ormanian, (5) followed by
Lepsius, presented it as 192,000; Theodik's almanac (6) as 197,000
and Eramian (7) as 180,000-200,000, while the Armenian Patriarchate
at Istanbul (8) estimated the 'sancak' of Van alone as 182,000.
These statistics concordantly attest that the Armenian population
of Van was about 190,000. I would therefore accept, as the most
credible estimate, the mean of the two extremes: 135,000.

TRADES AND CRAFTS OF ARMENIANS

The Armenians in the plains of Van, occupied in agriculture, contributed much to the rural economy of the province. In other parts
of the 'vilâyet' they were engaged in trades and various crafts and
professions. A. Dô informs us that there were 500 Armenian retailers in Van, and also many of the local craftsmen were Armenian.
He describes them with the following words:

> The Armenians of Van are noted for their ability. They are
> clever merchants and skilful craftsmen.... The trade of the
> province is almost completely in their hands. (9)

Lynch also states that most of the tradesmen and merchants were
Armenian. According to him the Armenian subject majority were hard-
working and created whatever wealth the city of Van possessed. He
adds:
> Commerce and industry find in the Armenian population of Van a
> soil in which they would flourish to imposing proportions under
> better circumstances.... (10)

At Başkale in Hakkâri, where Armenians had concentrated, they were
likewise engaged in different crafts and commerce.

SOURCES FOR THE ARMENIAN PARTICIPATION

In all the libraries of Britain, France, Austria, Syria, Lebanon and
Turkey that I have investigated, there is only one 'salname' of the
province of Van. This is the year-book of 1315H/1897-8 at the
University Library of Istanbul, No. 81042. (There is another copy
of the same annual in the Istanbul Municipal Library, 'Salnames',
No. 34/1.) In presenting the participation of Armenians in the
public life of Van I have used this 'salname' together with the
annuals of the 'vilâyet' of Erzurum for 1288H/1871-2, 1290H/1873-4,
1291H/1874-5 and 1292H/1875 when Van was a 'sancak' of that
province.

Why is it that only one year-book of Van is available? Perhaps
the Turkish authorities did not regularly publish annual statistics
because Van was the scene of Armenian troubles;   or, possibly, some
'salnames' were printed at first, but were later suppressed by the
Ottoman Government, or less probably lost to us through accident or
neglect.

CENTRES OF ARMENIAN PARTICIPATION

As the Armenians were the largest community in the town and 'kaza'
of Van, they played a conspicuous part in the work of the central
government there. Consul Taylor, followed by Lynch, has as we have
seen, estimated the number of Armenians in the 'kaza' of Van as
42,000, and Cuinet as 13,500. Other places in the 'sancak' of Van
where the Armenians were in the majority and contributed to the
public administration were the 'kazas' of Erciş and Adilcevaz.

It is of interest to note that the Armenians, in spite of the
fact that they were not so many in Hakkâri, have influenced public
life in this 'sancak' also. We find them in nearly every governmental department, although in a smaller proportion. Outlying
districts where the Armenian participation was considerable, were
the 'kazas' of Başkale and Özalp.

ARMENIAN PARTICIPATION IN VAN

1. The city of Van

In the central government of Van, the Armenians made a large contribution to public life. They had two members elected to the

administrative council, and also, from 1896 onwards, an ex officio
member, the assistant to the provincial governor, who from this date
always was Armenian. The assistants to the 'valis' of Van were:
Markos Aghabekian in 1896; Stephan Melikian from Istanbul, who
acted for seven months only, from April to October 1896, and
Yovhannes Ferit Boyadjian, 1896-1907. At the provincial headquarters about two Armenians were also elected as members to the
municipal council. In judicature, they were members of the judicial
inspectorate ('adliye müfettişligi') and the committee of public
prosecution. They also had members in the courts. Usually there
were four Armenian judges in the court of appeal, two in the civil,
and two in the criminal division, and two judges in the court of
first instance, one in each section. There were as many Armenians
as Muslim members in the commercial court. Trade and manufacture in
Van was mainly in the hands of Armenians. They contributed also to
the government's financial affairs, working in the control of
revenue and expenditure department, in the tax collection board, the
customs and the branch of the Agricultural Bank. In the state
tobacco monopoly they were employed as assistants to the accountants, as storekeepers and as workmen. In each financial department
normally there would be found about two Armenians.

In the provincial printing works, Armenians were mechanics and
compositors, and in the postal and telegraphic service they were
operators and translators. The police force had Armenian policemen
and superintendents of police, as well as clerks. These, however,
were kept in a minority compared with the Muslims. In 1893, Tigran
Amirdjanian, a learned Armenian with a good knowledge of Turkish and
French, was appointed head of the educational council and as provincial translator. It was the first time that an Armenian had held
this high position in Van.

2. The 'kazas' of Van

In the outer 'kazas' of the 'sancak' of Van, Armenians were mainly
occupied in political administration, finance and justice. In the
administrative councils there were generally two Armenian members,
as well as, after 1896, some ex officio members who were assistants
to the deputy-governors and the 'kaza'-governor. One or two
Armenian members were normally elected to the municipal councils, as
against two or three Muslims. In the courts of first instance, one
of the two members was always an Armenian. In public economy, the
Armenians worked in the tobacco monopoly, the taxation department
and on the tax collecting committee. At the time when Van was a
'sancak' to Erzurum, and when the treasury of the local administra-
tions of the 'kazas' was entrusted to the cashiers, the latter were
usually Armenian. Here is more evidence for the view that the Turks
relied on Armenians in monetary matters.

Armenians could be found in the police force, but this was un-
usual. They were very few in number and their influence was
negligible. In the 'nahiyes' of the 'kaza' of Van, namely at Erçek,
Timar and Huvasur, where the Armenian population was in the
majority, about two Armenians participated in the political administration, as elected members to the local councils.

3. The 'sancak' of Hakkâri

The 'sancak' of Hakkâri was inhabited mostly by Kurds. The
Armenians were concentrated in the 'kazas' of Hakkâri (Çölemerik)
and Başkale. In the central government of Hakkâri, Armenians had
two elected members on the administrative council and one or two on
the municipal council. There were Armenian officials in the judicature as well; one in the civil division of the court and another in
the criminal. In the revenue control Armenians worked as clerks,
and in the tobacco monopoly as assistants to the managers.

In the rest of the 'kazas' we find one Armenian official in each
department of the political administration; the court of first
instance; the tax-collection committee, and the police force. Only
occasionally were two Armenians, instead of one, elected as members
to the administrative councils.

COMPARATIVE NOTE: KURDISH AND SYRIAN PARTICIPATION

In the 'sancak' of Hakkâri, especially, lived many Kurds and Syrian
Christians, and naturally they took part in local government
affairs. One would expect that the Syrian officials should be
numerous and in many districts, but I could identify them only in
the 'kaza' of Özalp (Mahmudi), where they were included on the administrative and judicial councils, one in each department.

As to the Kurds, as far as I was able to differentiate them from
the Turks, I found them in Çölemerik, Başkale, Özalp, and even in
the 'kazas' of Gevaş and Şatak of the 'sancak' of Van. They acted,
though not steadily, in the administrative councils and on the
judicial courts, one being in each office.

A GENERAL VIEW OF ARMENIAN PARTICIPATION IN VAN

Van, from a political point of view, was a province to which the
Turks were sensitive and cautious, because like Erzurum it was not
very far from the vicinity of Russia; and second, the Armenians
were intending to try to obtain internal independence there with the
help of the Great Powers. In spite of this fact Armenians took a
reasonable part in the political, judicial and financial administration of the 'vilâyet'. However, whereas in other provinces they
worked also in technical, educational, agricultural, medical and
police departments, their contribution in Van in these fields of
public life was small. It is interesting to note that after the
Reforms of 1895-6, Armenian assistants were appointed to the 'valis'
of Van. But one can feel that Turks were not happy with this situation, and were tolerating these appointments only under European
scrutiny, because the office of two assistant-governors lasted only
for a very short period, and after the resignation of the third
(Yovhannes Ferit Boyadjian) no successors were appointed.

Some Armenian officials were also assigned to assist the deputy-
governors of the 'kazas', especially of Şatak and Gevaş, where the
Armenian inhabitants were in a majority from a racial point of
view.

SOME NOTABLE ARMENIANS IN THE PUBLIC LIFE OF VAN

AGHABEKIAN, Markos Efendi. For a short while at the beginning of
1896 he was the assistant to the 'vali' of Van.

AMIRDJANIAN, Tigran (c. 1835-97). Born and educated in Van, in 1860
he went to Istanbul and taught languages among Armenian families and
also in the Aramean school at Kadiköy. Returning to Van in 1867,
he continued to teach in the school of S. Yakob. In the days of the
'vali' Bahri Paşa, from 1893 to 1897, he was employed as the head of
the education council and as the provincial translator. He worked
under difficult conditions, because suspected documents found with
Armenians were brought to him to be checked or translated. For this
reason some Armenians attempted to take his life.

BOYADJIAN, Armenak. In 1905 and 1906 he was the assistant to the
deputy-governor of the 'kaza' of Gevaş.

BOYADJIAN, Ferit Yovhannes (1854-1948). A learned man (the brother
of Armenak Boyadjian), who for many years served the Ottoman Government. From the end of 1896 to 1907 he was the assistant to the
'vali' of Van.

KARAPET Efendi. He was the assistant to the deputy-governor of the
'kaza' of Şatak in 1902 and 1903.

MELIKIAN, Stephan Efendi (fl.c. 1880-96). Born in Istanbul, he was
educated in languages and the Ottoman legal code. For many years he
served the Ottoman embassies and consulates as dragoman and
ambassador and also became the governor of Archipelago. In April
1896 he was appointed assistant to the provincial governor of Van.
After seven months, when the 'vali', Şemseddîn Paşa was called back
by the Sublime Porte, he also resigned and went to Istanbul.
According to some sources, Stephan Efendi was suspected of being in
contact with the Armenian Socialist Huntchakian party.

TCHARUKHDJIAN, Nazareth. About 1908 he was a police superintendent
of the third grade in Van.

VARDAN Efendi. He was the assistant of the deputy-governor to the
'kaza' of Gevaş in 1902 and 1903.

Chapter 4

THE ARMENIANS OF ERZURUM

HISTORICAL SURVEY

The 'vilâyet' of Erzurum corresponds approximately to the High
Armenia or 'Karnoy ashkharh' (country of Karin) of ancient Armenia.
The city of Erzurum was called in Armenian Karin 'Qaghaq' (Karin
city) which became Qâlîqalâ in Arabic. In the eleventh century when
the Seljuks captured the town of Arzan (15 km north-west of Karin),
the population moved to Karin = Qâlîqalâ and gave it the name Arzân
al-Rûm, 'Arzân of the Romans', which through a misinterpretation
became Arz al-Rûm or Ard al-Rûm, 'the land of the Romans'.

The country of Karin (Erzurum) fell within the Roman share when
Armenia was divided between the Roman and Persian empires in 387.
In about 421 the town of Karin was renovated and called Theodosio-
polis, after the name of the emperor of that time. In 536, the
Emperor Justinian made the country of Karin a province and named it
First Armenia. About the middle of the seventh century it was
occupied by the Arabs, but it became the cause of much fighting between them and the Byzantines for the next three centuries. In 1049
the Seljuks conquered the province and destroyed the town of Arzan,
killing about 150,000 people. From 588H/1192 to 627H/1229-30
Erzurum was a separate Seljuk kingdom. In 1241 the Mongols invaded
the country and conquered it, and only in 878H/1473-4 as the result
of the battle of Tercan against the Aq-Qoyûnlu Uzun Hasan did the
Ottomans take possession of it under the Sultan Mehmed II. From
that time Erzurum formed an important 'paşalik' of the Ottoman
Empire. In 1877 it was occupied by the Russians, but they withdrew
after the Treaty of Berlin.

ADMINISTRATIVE STRUCTURE

The territorial content of the province of Erzurum in the second
half of the nineteenth century underwent a few changes. In 1865 it
was made an 'eyalet' (government-general) which included the whole
of the north-eastern part of Asia Minor. In 1292H/1875 this
'eyalet' was divided into six 'vilâyets', viz. Erzurum, Van,
Hakkâri, Bitlis, Hozat (Dersim) and Kars-Çildir. In 1888 by an

Imperial order Hakkâri was joined to the province of Van, and Hozat
to Elâzig (Ma'mûret ül-Azîz), while the 'sancak' of Bayburt, in
Erzurum, was attached to that of Erzincan. Consequently the
'vilâyet' of Erzurum had three 'sancaks' and nineteen 'kazas' as
follows.
The 'kazas' of the 'sancak' of Erzurum:
   Erzurum
   Ovacik
   Kigi
   Tercan
   Hinis
   Tortum
   Yusufeli (Kiskin)
   Hasankale (Pasinler)
The 'kazas' of the 'sancak' of Erzincan:
   Erzincan
   Refahiye
   Kuruçay
   Kemah
   Bayburt
   Ispir
The 'kazas' of the 'sancak' of Dogubayazit (Bayezit):
   Dogubayazit
   Diyadin
   Agri (Karakilise)
   Eleşkirt
   Tutak (Entap)

POPULATION

In 1862, the British Consul R.A.O. Dalyell reported that the population of the 'eyalet' of Erzurum (including Muş and Kars) was 732,458
of whom 25 per cent were Christian, most of these being Armenian.
(1) In 1869 the Consul J.G. Taylor assessed the Armenians of
Erzurum as 295,700 (287,000 Apostolic and 8,000 Catholic). (2) In
1888-9 when Erzurum had become a 'vilâyet', its population was
estimated by Fraşerî as 581,753, of whom 464,129 were said to be
Muslim and 109,835 Armenian. (3) At the same time (1890), Cuinet
(4) gave these detailed statistics for the province:

Armenians		
Apostolic	120,273	
Catholic	12,022	
Protestant	2,672	
		134,967
Greek Orthodox		3,725
Copts		16
Muslims		500,782
Jews		6
'Foreigners'		1,220
'Strangers'		4,986
Total		645,702

According to this author Armenians in the various 'sancaks' of the

province were as follows:
  'Sancak' of Erzurum
    Apostolic   77,476
    Catholic   10,180
    Protestant   2,288
  'Sancak' of Erzincan
    Apostolic   34,145
    Catholic   88
    Protestant   285
  'Sancak' of Dogubayazit
    Apostolic   8,652
    Catholic   1,754
    Protestant   99
Armenian sources as late as the first decade of this century give
different figures for the Armenian population. The Armenian
Patriarchate of Istanbul and the almanac of Theodik (5) estimate the
Armenian inhabitants of the province as 215,000. M. Ormanian, (6)
followed by Lepsius, presents these statistics totalling the
Armenian population as 203,400 for about 1900:
  Erzurum
    Erzurum   85,000
    Hasankale   10,500
    Tercan   15,000
    Kigi   25,000
                                135,500
  Erzincan
    Erzincan   25,500
    Bayburt   17,000
    Kemah   10,200
                                 52,700
  Dogubayazit   15,200
                               _____
              Total   203,400
We can conclude that the mean of the figures given by Fraşerî,
Cuinet, Ormanian and Lepsius, for Armenians, and the total popula-
tion of Erzurum, i.e. 150,000 and 624,385, is the most realistic
approximation possible. This means that 25 per cent of the total
population were Armenians, which agrees with the figures given by
Dalyell.

TRADES AND CRAFTS OF ARMENIANS

The Armenians in the country districts of Erzurum were occupied in
agriculture, but not many of them actually owned land. Heavy taxation, banditry and oppression by Turkish and Kurdish chiefs had
deprived the Armenian villagers of their hereditary estates. Therefore those who had no plot or farm of their own worked on government
land or for other landowners. After the payment of the government
tithe, the remainder of the crop was divided between proprietor and
the villagers in varying proportions according to the terms of their
agreement.
     The majority of Armenians were, however, concentrated in the
towns and occupied in trade and various crafts. In 1862 Consul
Dalyell reported:

The mercantile class in the towns [in the 'eyalet' of Erzurum] is accordingly, principally Christian, who generally own their own houses, or shops; but it is to be observed that it is by no means rare in this part of Turkey for Christians to possess even considerable land property. (7)

Through Erzurum ran a road of great strategic and commercial importance. This was the historic trade route from Trebizond to Tabriz. As a result, Erzurum was a busy centre of commerce, and the Armenians, together with the Greek and Persian merchants, took an active part in its trade. A. Dô gives his eye-witness account of the share which Armenians had in the trade and handicrafts of the province. Speaking especially of the city of Erzurum, he says:

The Armenians deal mainly with commerce and handicrafts. The crafts are well developed here. In Erzurum there are more than 3,000 shops and taverns, of which nearly half belong to Armenians. About 500 of these Armenians are retail dealers; some are big merchants who have commercial relations with Istanbul and other towns. More than 1,000 people are occupied in crafts of which the most advanced - masonry - supports many Armenian families not only in the towns, but also in the villages on the plain. (8)

CENTRES OF ARMENIAN PARTICIPATION

Many Armenians lived in the centres of the province, and most of them were settled in the 'sancak' of Erzurum itself. According to the statistics of Cuinet (9) 89,944 out of the total Armenian population of 134,967 inhabited the 'sancak' of Erzurum. From this it follows that the Armenians took a comparatively large part in the public administration of the central 'sancak'.

In the other two 'sancaks', the Armenians contributed to public life especially in the town of Erzincan, and in the 'kazas' of Kuruçay and Kemah in the 'sancak' of Erzinçan, and in the 'kazas' of Dogubayazit, Karakilise and Eleşkirt of the 'sancak' of Dogubayazit.

MAIN FIELDS OF ARMENIAN PARTICIPATION

The main fields of Armenian participation were those of political administration, finance, and judicature. In the town of Erzurum, where the government headquarters were situated, the Armenians contributed to the public life on a large scale. The bishops of the Apostolic and Catholic communities were ex officio members of the local administrative council, and there were two other Armenian members elected from the respected or educated people. Usually two Armenian members were elected to the municipal council, as against between four and six Turks. In the other parts of the 'vilâyet', the spiritual heads of the Armenians were ex officio members of the administrative councils in the 'kazas' of Ovacik, Kigi, Tercan and Hasankale in Erzurum; Bayburt and Ispir in Erzincan, and Dogubayazit, Agri (Karakilise) and Eleşkirt in Dogubayazit. In each 'kaza', apart from the ex officio members, two Armenians were generally elected also. On the municipal councils the Armenians had

between one and three, but normally two members, elected;   on the
whole this was fewer than the Turks.

In the financial affairs of the 'vilâyet', Armenians, being ex-
perienced traders, played a noteworthy role. They worked in the
departments of the treasury, the control of revenue, the tobacco
monopoly, the public debt administration, the chamber of commerce
and the branch of the Agricultural Bank. They were from one to
three in number and were employed as clerks, accountants, cashiers,
storekeepers. As a rule about six out of the eight or nine
officials in the tobacco monopoly were Armenian. In the judicature,
at the centre of Erzurum, Armenians were included in the courts of
first instance, appeal and of commerce. They acted both in the
civil and criminal departments, as judges, being two, but more often
one, in each division. In the court of commerce, there were
normally two or more Armenian members, sometimes accompanied by a
Greek. The situation was much the same at the centres of the
'sancaks' of Erzincan and Dogubayazit. In each of the outlying
'kazas', the Armenians were usually represented by one member in the
court of first instance, which was the only department of justice.

OTHER FIELDS OF ARMENIAN PARTICIPATION

Other aspects of Armenian activity in government departments were in
the offices of the secretariat, engineering, the public health service, the agricultural inspectorate, the education committee, and
the police force. This participation took place mainly in the
centres of the 'sancaks'. Armenians served in the departments of
engineering and public works as engineers and foremen;   in the
postal and telegraphic service as operators, and in the press, as
compositors and mechanics. In secretarial work it is notable that
the 'vilâyet' translator was often Armenian. Armenian translators
were employed in the postal and telegraphic service. Armenian
clerks worked in the chief secretariat, the land registry and the
registry of births.

With regard to agricultural participation we find Armenian
officials principally engaged as forestry inspectors. In education
Armenians co-operated with the Turks in the education councils and
committees. It is interesting to see that after the Reforms of 1896
the Armenian language was introduced into the syllabus of the
secondary school in the town of Erzurum.

There were occasionally one or two Armenian policemen in the
police force. At the centre of the 'vilâyet' there were also sometimes one or two assistant superintendents. Again at the centre in
the city of Erzurum itself, Armenians were appointed as municipal
doctors, but not regularly.

COMPARATIVE NOTE: GREEK PARTICIPATION

The Greek community of Erzurum was quite small. Cuinet records
their total number as about 3,700. (10) Greek participation
accordingly was not large. They served the public life sometimes
and were very few in number. Greek officials took part in public

administration in the 'sancaks' of Erzurum and Erzincan, and especially in the centres of these districts. They acted in the
administrative councils, in the courts of justice and commerce,
tobacco monopoly, public debt administration, and postal and telegraphic service. Their co-operation is noticeable in public health
as well, particularly as chemists. As concerns their number, there
was not usually more than one in each department.

A GENERAL VIEW OF ARMENIAN PARTICIPATION IN ERZURUM

Erzurum, according to the Armenian sources, was the 'vilâyet' where
the Armenians were most numerous. Consequently one could expect a
greater participation from them in the public life of the province.
But in fact this is not so. Their part in public administration was
neither very large nor very steady. The 'vilâyet' of Diyarbakir,
for example, presents a contrasting situation.
   Why was the participation of Armenians in the public life of
Erzurum thus limited? I should think, because this province
bordered on Russia, and the Turks were very cautious concerning its
security and preservation. Still, the Armenians took a considerable
part especially in the administrative councils, courts of justice,
and public debt, being quite influential in the latter. They
usually held moderate offices, such as consultant members, cashiers,
clerks, as artisans in various technical departments, and as
physicians or chemists. Sometimes they were also appointed to
higher positions, such as heads of the public debt administration,
chamber of commerce, municipal council, and as provincial
translators.

SOME NOTABLE ARMENIANS IN THE PUBLIC LIFE OF ERZURUM

AYDJIAN, L. He was an assistant to the 'vali' of Erzurum.
BALLARIAN, Hamazasp. In 1876 he was elected deputy for Erzurum in
the Ottoman Parliament at Istanbul. His brother, M. Ballarian, was
a banker in Erzurum.
BILLORIAN, Andranik. He was an assistant to the provincial governor
of Erzurum.
DARPASIAN, Derenik. The son of Yovhannes who himself for a while
was the cashier of the taxation department. Derenik learned good
Turkish and became the notary of the census office. Profiting from
the advantages of his office he greatly helped his compatriots by
providing them with new identity cards and travel documents.
DER-NERSESIAN, Khatchadur (1810-95). Born at Bitlis, he became a
merchant and was appreciated even by the Persian government. He
directed the customs first at Erzurum, and then in Van. 'For many
years' he also participated in the administrative council of
Erzurum. In 1877 he was employed by the Russian Consulate at
Erzurum as translator. In the same year he was elected deputy in
the Ottoman Parliament at Istanbul. When the Parliament was dis-
missed, he settled down at Istanbul. For his public services he was
given decoration by the Sublime Porte.
HEKIMIAN, Michayel Efendi. From about 1903 to 1906 he was a provincial translator.

KARADJIAN, Daniel. In 1876 he was elected by the Armenian community
of Erzurum a deputy in the Ottoman Parliament at Istanbul.
MEGUERDITCH Efendi. He was the chief clerk in the public debt
administration of Erzurum from 1903 to 1906.
MELIKIAN, Dr Karapet (1883-1915). Born at Arapkir, he studied in a
local school and then in the Euphrates College of Harput. In 1902
he went to Beirut and studied medicine. In 1907 getting his M.D.
degree, he went to Kigi and was employed as a municipal doctor.
PAPAZIAN, Dr Enovch (?-1913). He was a chief doctor in the army
medical corps at Erzurum.
SHABANIAN, Krikor (Gregor) Efendi (1835-1908). In 1865 he was
elected a member of the administrative council of Erzurum, and in
1885 he held the post of the director of public debt administration.
About 1893 he was appointed assistant to the public prosecutor, but
soon resigned.
YARMAYAN, Dr Minas (?-1915). Originally from Tokat, he studied
first in the College of Merzifon and then went to Beirut to study
medicine. In 1904 he graduated from the American University of
Beirut, and returning home he served in the military Aziziye
hospital at Erzincan.

Chapter 5

THE ARMENIANS OF TREBIZOND

HISTORICAL SURVEY

Trebizond (Gr. Trapezous, Arm. Trapizon, Arb. Atrâbazund and
Tarâbazunda, Otto.Turk. Tarabzûn or Tarabzôn, and Mod.Turk. Trabzon)
in the early centuries of the Christian era was a region of the
Roman, and later of the Byzantine Empire. After the seventh century
Arabs penetrated the area, inhabited and traded there. During the
Arab period, until the invasion of Seljuks, Trebizond became an important centre of commerce, from where Byzantine merchandise was
carried to the Muslim world, through Erzurum. In 1204, Alexis
founded the Comneni Empire and made Trebizond his capital. This
tiny empire had a short life, for in 1214 when the Seljuk Sultan
Alâ' al-Dîn Kayqubâdh captured Sinope, the Emperor of Trebizond was
forced to recognize his suzerainty. And in 1240 when the Mongols
subjugated the Seljuks, the Emperor Manuel admitted himself to be a
vassal of the Mongol Empire. Until the middle of the fifteenth century, the country flourished again economically.
    From the beginning of the fourteenth century Trebizond was
attacked by the Turkomans who came to possess the strongholds on the
mountains in the hinterland. In 865H/1460-1, the Ottoman Sultan
Mehmed II, marching through Kastamonu and Sinope, conquered
Trebizond. Many of the inhabitants of the town, the majority most
probably Greek with an Armenian minority, were transported to
Istanbul, and only a remnant were allowed to live in the suburbs.
This was the last Byzantine citadel to fall to the Ottomans. Under
Ottoman rule, Trebizond became a centre of an 'eyalet', and in the
nineteenth century of a 'vilâyet', but it never recovered its former
great commercial activity.
    From the Armenian point of view, Armenians had lived on the
coasts of the Black Sea, in the regions of Trebizond and Rize
(Lazistan) for centuries. In 536 the Emperor Justinian included
Trebizond in First Armenia. After the seventh century, the Armenian
Paulician sectarians took shelter there. In 788 when the Armenians
were suffering from the Arab atrocities in their homeland, 12,000 of
them escaped to Pontus. The Emperor Constantine VI (780-97) wel-
comed the notables into his palace and army, and settled the rest of

the people 'in good and fertile country', actually in Rize (the
former 'sancak' of Lazistan). (1)   The leaders of this emigration
were the prince Shapuh Amatuni and his son Hamam, after whose name
the district where the Armenians settled was called Hamamshên, i.e.
'built by Hamam', and later Hamshên or Hamşên (now Hemşin).   After
the fall of the Armenian kingdom of Bagratuni, many people were
spread abroad, of whom some came to join their compatriots in
Trebizond.   The Armenians of Hamşên in the eighteenth century were
converted by force into Islam, but they preserved certain Christian
customs and their native tongue, (2) as did the Greeks who shared
the same fate.

ADMINISTRATIVE STRUCTURE

The province of Trebizond was divided into four 'sancaks' and in-
cluded 22 'kazas'.
The 'kazas' of the 'sancak' of Trebizond:
    Trebizond
    Sürmene
    Akçaabât (Polathane)
    Vakfikebir
    Görele
    Tirebolu
    Giresun
    Ordu
The 'kazas' of the 'sancak' of Samsun (Canik):
    Samsun
    Fatsa
    Ünye
    Terme
    Çarşanba
    Bafra
The 'kazas' of the 'sancak' of Rize (Lazistan):
    Rize
    Of
    Pazar
    Hopa
The 'kazas' of the 'sancak' of Gümüşane (Gümüşhane):
    Gümüşane
    Torul
    Şiran
    Kelkit
The last two 'kazas', viz. Şiran and Kelkit, were formerly included
in the province of Erzurum, but in March 1888 were attached to
Trebizond.

POPULATION

The general population of Trebizond in the second half of the nineteenth century according to Cuinet (3) was as follows:

Armenians (4)
Apostolic	44,100
Catholic	2,300
Protestant	800

	47,200
Orthodox Greeks	193,000
Latins	400
Muslims	
Turk	691,700
Laz (5)	55,000
Circassian	60,000
	806,700
Jews	400

Total	1,047,700

Fraşerî (6) in 1874 presents the total of the Armenians in the
'vilâyet' as 52,349, and some years later the provincial year-book
of 1320H/1902-3 gives the following estimate: (7)

'Sancak' of Trebizond	28,707
Samsun	20,184
Gümüşane	1,767
Rize	20

Total	50,678

It will be observed from these statistics that the Armenians of
Trebizond were about 51,000-52,000, and therefore more than the
number given by Cuinet. The Armenian sources, anyhow, record dif-
ferent figures. Theodik's almanac (8) accounts the total of the
Armenian community as 65,000, while Ormanian, (9) followed by
Lepsius, records these statistics:

Apostolic	50,000
Catholic	2,500
Protestant	1,000

Total	53,500

TRADES AND PROFESSIONS OF ARMENIANS

The Armenians in Trebizond were occupied in agriculture, handicrafts
and manufacture, and especially in trade. In parts of the province
where the soil was suitable, they cultivated fruit and cereals and
bred cattle; but as they were rather concentrated in littoral towns
they dealt mainly with commerce and crafts. (10) The Armenians were
also engaged in the various professions, particularly in medicine.
Many of them, having studied in the schools of Istanbul and Paris,
served the people as doctors and chemists. The provincial year-book
of 1322H/1904-5 records the names of the following Armenians who
were apothecaries at Trebizond:

Karapet (Garabed) Tchirakian
Karapet Surmalian
Stephan Surmalian
Boghos Zahigöy

CENTRES OF ARMENIAN PARTICIPATION

The Armenians of Trebizond were more influential at the headquarters of the 'sancaks'. Since about half of the Armenian population of the 'vilâyet' lived in the 'sancak' of Trebizond itself, they played an important role in public administration. Apart from the centres, Armenians worked in different governmental departments of the 'kazas' Ordu, Giresun, Tirebolu and Görele of the 'sancak' of Trebizond; in the 'kazas' Fatsa, Ünye, Çarşanba in Samsun, and in the 'sancak' of Gümüşane, in the 'kazas' of Kelkit and Şiran. In Rize the Armenian officials on paper were very few, for it was not possible to identify the islamized Armenians, since, if there were any, these would appear with Muslim names.

MAIN FIELDS OF ARMENIAN PARTICIPATION

Trebizond is the only province within the limits of this study where Greek influence in public life was stronger than Armenian. The reason was that among the Christian population the Greeks were in a majority. It is interesting to note, however, that in the 'sancaks' of Trebizond, Samsun and Gümüşane, the Armenians were also employed in many governmental departments, although not in equal number with the Greeks. The main fields of Armenian participation were in political administration, justice and finance. In the administrative councils there were one or two Armenian elected members. In the centre of Trebizond, as well as in its 'kazas' Ordu, Görele, Giresun, Akçaabât, and in the headquarters of Samsun, there was also an ex officio member who was the Apostolic bishop of that district. In the centre of Trebizond and Samsun, only the Armenian Catholic vicars were also ex officio members. In the 'nahiyes' an Armenian was usually included on the administrative council. In a high position we find a certain Karapet Efendi as assistant to the governor of the 'sancak' of Samsun in 1319H/1901-2. In the municipal councils there were one or two Armenian elected members. At Fatsa, in Samsun, between 1298H/1880-1 and 1309H/1891-2 the mayor was an Armenian.

In the judicature, particularly at the courts, the Armenians made a considerable contribution. In the centres of the 'sancaks' of Trebizond, Samsun and Gümüşane, both in the courts of first instance and appeal, and of commerce, there were usually one or two Armenian members. In the rest of the 'kazas' in every court of first instance an Armenian would be found. In some of the 'kazas' Greeks were influential and in others Armenians. Outside the courts, Armenians also served the public notary and the trial committee ('enctmen-i adliye') as assistants to the inspectors.

In the financial affairs of the government, Armenians took a large part, and their activity was regular especially in the centre of the province. The Armenian officials were members (one to three in number) of the taxation department and revenue and expenditure control, the estimates committee, the Ottoman and Agricultural Banks, and chambers of commerce and agriculture. They also shared in a large proportion, and in responsible positions, the work of the tobacco monopoly and public debt. For example, from 1900 onwards,

the head of the Ottoman debt administration was usually an Armenian.
In the other 'kazas' of the 'vilâyet', the Armenians likewise took
a notable part in the field of finance. They were employed in tax
collection, estimates committee, tobacco monopoly, the banks,
chamber of commerce and in public debt administration. As to their
proportion, there were generally two in each department. The functions which they filled were usually the offices of accountant,
cashier, clerk and storekeeper. Trebizond, situated on the Black
Sea with a bad though viable harbour, was a busy port. There were
resident agents for Turkish, French, Russian, Italian and Greek
shipping interests. The Armenians, by virtue of their knowledge of
European languages, were employed in these agencies as managers or
managers in charge and as clerks. The French, Russian and Italian
companies of Trebizond, Ordu, Giresun, Samsun and Ünye entrusted
their agencies to the Armenian officials.

OTHER FIELDS OF ARMENIAN PARTICIPATION

Other fields of public life in which the Armenians acted were
engineering, the postal and telegraphic service, agriculture, public
health, education and the police force. Their participation in
these spheres of public administration was not very influential
since they were few in number. At the town of Trebizond, in the
headquarters of the province, there were Armenians in the engineering department, as engineers and foremen; in the public works
board; in the postal and telegraphic service as operators in the
foreign communication section; and in the press as mechanics and
compositors. Armenian officials were employed as well on the agricultural board and education council, in the chief secretariat and
land registry board, and in the police force. The municipal doctor
was sometimes Armenian.
    In the rest of the 'kazas' of Trebizond itself and of the
'sancak' Samsun, Armenians were included on the agricultural and
forestry board, and in the municipality as advisory members and
doctors, in the public works, postal and telegraphic service, and in
the chief secretariat. While in the central provincial government's
departments the Armenians were one to three in number, in the
'kazas' there was usually only one in each office. In the 'sancaks'
of Gümüşane and particularly Rize we scarcely ever find Armenians
out of the affairs of political administration, justice and finance.

COMPARATIVE NOTE: GREEK PARTICIPATION

As has been mentioned, Trebizond is the only 'vilâyet' of Eastern
Anatolia where the Greeks were more influential than the Armenians.
Comparing the participation of these two Christian nations in the
public life of the province, one notices that the Greeks made a
larger and steadier contribution. Since they were in the majority
we find them more numerous in the government departments. They
sometimes held high positions as mayors and administrators of the
tobacco monopoly. There was even a Greek assistant to the provincial governor, between 1286H/1869-70 and 1288H/1871-2. On the

other hand it is noticeable that in the judiciary the Armenians were predominant. The probable reason for this was that the Turks desired to counterbalance the influence of Greeks, or there may simply have been more law officials available among the Armenians. From a geographical point of view, while the Armenians were only included in the departments of political administration, finance and justice, in the 'sancak' of Gümüşane, the Greeks also acted in agriculture, technical crafts, public health service and education.

In the central government of the province, at Trebizond, the Greeks took part in political administration, judicature, finance, agriculture and technical works. There were Greek members of the administrative council, one ex officio and one elected, and in the municipality there were usually two. In the courts of first instance, appeal and of commerce there was one Greek in each section. In financial spheres they worked in tax collection, the estimates committee, tobacco monopoly, Ottoman and Agricultural Bank branches, and public debt administration. As for education, they were sometimes employed on the education committee and in the secondary school. They made an important contribution to engineering and public works as engineers, and in the postal and telegraphic service as operators.

In the other 'kazas' of Trebizond, Samsun and Gümüşane, the Greeks likewise influenced the political administration, justice, finance, public health and mechanical affairs. There were two Greek members in the administrative councils, one ex officio and another elected, and in the municipal council, one or two. In the courts of first instance there was a Greek member, who was sometimes replaced by an Armenian. Greek officials were also members of the boards of agriculture and the branches of the Agricultural Bank and of the tax collecting committee. The municipal doctors were often Greeks. They outnumbered others in the tobacco monopoly and one Greek would usually be found in the postal and telegraphic service, and one or two in the public works.

A GENERAL VIEW OF ARMENIAN PARTICIPATION IN TREBIZOND

To summarize the Armenian participation in the public life of Trebizond, we can say that on the whole the Armenians were treated fairly. In spite of the fact that they were not in a majority, they were included in most of the government departments of the 'sancaks' of Trebizond, Samsun and Gümüşane and they were especially influential in political administration, justice and finance. Armenian officials were generally employed as advisory members in various offices, as lawyers, clerks, cashiers, translators, doctors and mechanics.

Why should the Armenians have been better treated in Trebizond than in the inland provinces, where they were more numerous? Perhaps it was because the western countries and Russia had consulates there, and perhaps also because this 'vilâyet', being not so far from the Sublime Porte, was influenced by its control. It is possible that the caprices of the 'vali' and robbery by bandits were thus to a certain extent restrained. No doubt, that, had the other provinces also been as well governed and the life of the population secure, the Armenians could have been spared massacres and Turkey could have retained the services of this industrious people for her own development.

SOME NOTABLE ARMENIANS IN THE PUBLIC LIFE OF TREBIZOND

ANTON Efendi. He was a provincial translator from 1902 to 1908.
ARSLANIAN, Levon. He was a municipal doctor from about 1906 to 1915.
ASLANIAN, Oskan Efendi. He was a provincial forestry inspector in 1908.
FIKRI, Kevork (Georg) Efendi. He was the head of the commercial court and assistant to the general judicial inspector, from 1900 to 1908.
KARAPET (Garabed) Efendi. He was the assistant to the governor of the 'sancak' of Samsun in 1319H/1901-2.
KHORASIAN, Eduard Efendi. He was a chief engineer about 1870.
SHABANIAN, Krikor Efendi. He was director of the public debt administration, from 1900 to 1906.

Chapter 6

THE ARMENIANS OF SIVAS

HISTORICAL SURVEY

Sivas (class. Megalopolis and Sebastia, Arm. Sebastia and later
Svaz, Arb. Sîwâs, Ott.Turk. Sîvâs) in the Byzantine period was in-
cluded in Second Armenia.   In 1021-2 it was given by the Emperor
Basil II to the Armenian king Seneqerim Ardzruni in exchange for the
province Vaspurakan (Van and its surroundings) for defence purposes.
About 14,000 families followed their king and settled in Sivas. (1)
In 451H/1059 the Seljuks, under the command of Samûkh, invaded
Sivas, and sacked it, massacring many of the population and burning
the town.   The sons of Seneqerim, Atom and Apusahl escaped to
Gabadonia (Develi).   After eight days the Seljuks withdrew, but at
the battle of Malazgirt, on 26 August 1071 Cappadocian Armenia fell
into their hands.   Subsequently Sivas was ruled for a period by
Turkoman dynasties, and in 1398 was taken over by the Ottoman Sultan
Yildirim Bayezid I.   In 1400 the Mongol Emperor Tîmûr attacked Sivas
with huge armies, undermined the walls of the town, captured the
people and put many of them to death.   He was particularly cruel
towards the Armenian regiment which had strongly resisted him on
behalf of the Ottomans.   However the Mongols' domination in Asia
Minor did not last long and on their withdrawal in 1403 the Ottomans
again brought Sivas and its adjacent regions under their rule.
Hereafter Sivas became the centre of an 'eyalet', including the
'sancaks' of Amasya, Çorum, Bozok, Samsun, Divrigi and Arapkir.   In
the nineteenth century, when the new provincial constitution was
proclaimed, Sivas formed a 'vilâyet' covering the 'sancaks' of
Amasya, Tokat and Şebinkarahisar.

ADMINISTRATIVE STRUCTURE

The 'vilâyet' of Sivas was divided into four 'sancaks', Sivas,
Tokat, Amasya and Şebinkarahisar, and had twenty-six 'kazas' as the
following.
The 'kazas' of the 'sancak' of Sivas:
   Sivas
   Zara (Koçkiri)

Divrigi
Şarkişla (Tonus)
Gürün
Darende
Hafik
Yildizeli
Pinarbaşi (Aziziye)
The 'kazas' of the 'sancak' of Tokat:
Tokat
Erbaa
Zile
Niksar
The 'kazas' of the 'sancak' of Amasya:
Amasya
Merzifon
Vezirköprü
Osmancik
Gümüşhaciköy
Ladik
Havza
Mecidözü
The 'kazas' of the 'sancak' of Şebinkarahisar (Şarkikarahisar):
Şebinkarahisar
Mesudiye (Hamidiye)
Koyulhisar
Suşehri
Alucra

POPULATION

The total population of the 'vilâyet' of Sivas in the second half of
the nineteenth century according to V. Cuinet (1890) was 1,086,015
of whom 170,433 were Armenian: (2)

Armenians
    Apostolic   129,523
    Protestant   30,433
    Catholic   10,477
                        170,433
Orthodox Greeks   76,068
Muslims
    Turk, Turkoman
      and Circassian 559,680
    Kizilbash   279,834
                     839,514

        Total   1,086,015

The same figures are given by Fraşerî (3) in 1893-4, but with the
addition of 400 Jews to the total. The provincial year-book of
1321H/1903-4 estimates the number of the Armenians at about 133,700.
According to Cuinet the Armenians of Sivas lived in different
'sancaks' of the 'vilâyet', as follows:

  'Sancak' of Sivas   63,868
         Tokat   37,919

Amasya   50,600
Şebinkarahisar   18,046

In connection with the Armenian population of Sivas, the Armenian
authors present different numbers to the above quoted figures.
Gabikian estimates the total as 350,284, (4) Ormanian as 200,000,
while the almanac of Theodik gives 225,000. (5)   According to
Ormanian, (6) the Armenians of Sivas were concentrated in different
districts of the province as follows.

Sivas:	Apostolic	80,000	
	Protestant	1,000	
	Catholic	5,000	
			86,000
Divrigi:	Apostolic	11,000	
	Protestant	300	
			11,300
Gürün:	Apostolic	17,000	
	Protestant	1,000	
	Catholic	500	
			18,500
Darende:	Apostolic	7,000	
			7,000
Tokat:	Apostolic	21,000	
	Protestant	500	
	Catholic	2,000	
			23,500
Amasya:	Apostolic	25,000	
	Protestant	3,000	
	Catholic	500	
			28,500
Sebinkarahisar:	Apostolic	25,000	
	Protestant	200	
			25,200

In my opinion the total recorded by Ormanian for the Armenian population of Sivas is a moderate and reasonable one in comparison with
the figures of Turkish and other Armenian sources, the first of
which have apparently under-estimated and the latter exaggerated the
numbers according to their inclinations or interests.

TRADES AND PROFESSIONS OF ARMENIANS

The Armenian peasants in Sivas were employed in agriculture. They
had obtained improved implements for cultivation. Many others were
occupied in various handicrafts, mainly in the printing of cotton
hangings, making belts, the blacksmith's art, painting and dye-
works, watch-repairings, sewing, shoe-making, carpentry and mason's
work, and in carpet and textile weaving. Nathanian, speaking of the
centre province Sivas, records thus:
  In Sivas there are about thirty handicrafts which appertain in
  the main to the Armenians. In the town of Sivas there are also
  large markets divided into parts which include many shops of all
  sorts of merchandise, about 1,200, large and small. The craftsmen mostly are Armenian, and particularly the traders. (7)
More wealthy Armenians were engaged in commerce and money-exchange.

The trade of the province was principally in their hands and they
were regarded as shrewd merchants. Cuinet says:
    Pour la plupart, les Arméniens de cette province s'occupent de
    prêts d'argent, de change de monnaies et d'autres trafics
    semblables. (8)
A much populated Armenian district was the 'sancak' of Tokat.
According to Alboyadjian the Armenians were generally concentrated
in the towns, and were mostly occupied in arts and trades. The same
author attests the following concerning the town of Tokat itself:
    The main houses of commerce and haberdashery or of import and
    export of articles by retail and wholesale belonged to the
    Armenians. For this reason they were not a contemptible and
    neglectable element in the economic life of the town. (9)
It is noticeable that the Armenians also contributed, officially and
unofficially, to the public hygiene of Sivas. There were many
chemists and physicians serving different parts of the province of
whom Sarkis Parseghian, Hindlian, Levon Hiwsisian, Miridjan
Karmirian, Karapet Pashayan and Yaruthiwn Vezneyan can be named.

CENTRES OF ARMENIAN PARTICIPATION

In Sivas the Armenians took part in the public administration of
almost all the districts of the province. Their participation, however, was larger in the 'sancak' of Sivas where the government headquarters were situated. In the rest of the 'vilâyet' particular
centres of Armenian contribution were the 'kazas' of Merzifon,
Vezirköprü, Ladik, Mecidözü in the 'sancak' of Amasya; Zile and
Niksar in the 'sancak' of Tokat, and the 'kaza' Suşehri in
Şebinkarahisar.

THE MAIN FIELDS OF ARMENIAN PARTICIPATION

The Armenians in the central government of the 'sancaks' took part
in most public affairs, and their influence was stronger in the
centres than in the other 'kazas'. The main fields of Armenian
participation were the departments of political administration,
finance, justice and the secretariat. In the administrative councils of the central 'kazas' of Sivas, Tokat, Amasya and Şebinkarahisar, there were usually two Armenian elected members. After the
Reforms there were also two ex officio members, one Apostolic and
one Catholic. At Sivas four Armenians were elected to the central
municipality, while in the other municipal councils two or three
Armenian members were elected. In the sphere of finance the
Armenians were employed in many offices, particularly at Sivas.
They served the control of revenue and expenditure, treasury, the
chamber of commerce, tobacco monopoly, the branches of the Agricultural and Ottoman Banks, public debt, administration of tithes
and sheep, customs, and the taxation board. There were also
Armenians in the salt administration who worked as clerks, weighing-
officials and storekeepers. The proportions in which the Armenians
participated were not very constant. In these financial departments
they varied in number from one to four.
    In the judicature of the headquarters of the province the

Armenians held offices in both sections, civil and criminal, of the courts of first instance and of appeal. They seem to have been influential in the courts of appeal, having two or three judges in each. In the departments of first instance there were only one or two Armenians, but in the commercial court they were given a large part and sometimes even the presidency. We find Armenian officials also employed in the trial commissions and as lawyers. As to the secretariat the Armenians, due to their good knowledge of Turkish and other languages, served in many offices, viz. chief secretariat, land registry, municipality's secretariat, registry of real estates, secretariat of revenue control, and the postal and telegraphic service. In these departments they were usually two or three in number.

In the outer 'kazas' of the province, the Armenian officials were not so numerous as in the centres, as the number of government offices and of their personnel was by comparison limited. One or two were, however, elected members to the administrative councils, and two or three to the municipalities. The spiritual heads of the Apostolic communities were sometimes included on the administrative councils as ex officio members. In the government of 'nahiyes', there were Armenian administrators, assistants to the administrators, and members to the local councils, but they did not hold a predominant position compared with the Turks. Armenians contributed more to the financial affairs of the 'kazas' than to any other circles. They were in particular employed in the tobacco monopoly, the branches of the Agricultural Bank, and in the control of revenue. The district managers of the tobacco monopoly were often Armenian. Other departments where they co-operated with the Ottoman Government were the treasury, tax collection, public debt administration, and the chamber of commerce. Their share was not very steady and sometimes they were two or three in number, and sometimes only one.

In the judicature of the 'kazas' the part of Armenians was limited to the courts of first instance. They always had one member, and sometimes two, in the courts, but naturally they could not guarantee a right judgment in the cases of the Armenian communities since the Turks were more numerous. They numbered three or four, apart from the president who was always a Turk. In respect of the secretariat there were usually three Armenian officials employed in the chief secretariat and a general average of two in the land registry.

OTHER FIELDS OF ARMENIAN PARTICIPATION

In the agriculture of this province, particularly of the central 'sancaks', Armenians were employed by the forestry board, by the inspectorate board of agriculture and crafts, and as forest rangers. They normally numbered between one and three but on the board of agriculture the Armenian membership reached up to six persons.

In technical affairs Armenian officials also took a notable part. They worked as engineers and foremen in the road and building office, the engineering department and the public works; as mechanics in the postal and telegraphic service, and as compositors

in the press. The chief compositors were usually Armenian. It is
of interest that the 'vilâyet' press at Sivas had a section for
Armenian printing. The provincial annual of 1301H/1883-4 gives the
names of two compositors of Armenian, viz. Meguerditch Efendi and
his assistant Hayk Efendi. Nathanian who in 1875/6 visited Sivas,
records the following about the printing house:

> A winding path through some willows leads from the upper part to
> Sivas, at the western entrance of which on the right side can be
> seen a one-storeyed barracks built in stone of medium size. On
> the left there is a marble fountain of sweet water. The govern-
> ment house, a large building, is erected a little beyond where
> the 'vali' of the province resides and has a newly established
> printing office under the management of Andranik Efendi
> Vardanian, who also edits the local Turkish newspaper 'Sîvâs'.
> (10)

From different sources we know that Vardanian Efendi had an Armenian
press of his own, from 1871 to 1875, where, among other things, he
published the 'Prayer Book' (1875) of the Armenian Church.
Apparently in 1875/6, when he was appointed by the government as the
manager of its printing office, he gave up his own work.

The Armenians also contributed to the local state industry as
technicians and managers for the textile, mining, leather, and
timber boards. In the public health service the Armenians, together
with the Greeks, took a considerable part as municipal doctors,
surgeons and chemists. In the infirmary of Sivas the Armenians
rendered good service as well. As to education, we find Armenians
in the schools as teachers, and one or two acting as consultants on
the education committees. At Sivas Armenians taught in the preparatory and the girls' schools. In the latter Iskuhi Hanim and
Elbiz Hanim taught carpet-making.

Armenians were rarely employed in the police force and even then
were only one or two in number. In the 'kazas' and 'nahiyes' they
were used as policemen, but in the central 'sancaks' as assistant
superintendents and police sergeants also.

COMPARATIVE NOTE: GREEK PARTICIPATION

The Greeks in Sivas did not take a large part in the public administration. Their participation was considerable only at the centres
of the 'sancaks', as well as in the 'kazas' Merzifon, Ladik and
Havza in Amasya, at Niksar in the 'sancak' of Tokat, and in the
'kazas' of Hamidiye and Alucra in Şebinkarahisar. Greeks were included on the administrative councils, education committees and
judicial courts. They were employed also as provincial translators
and as clerks in the chief secretariat. Their share was greater in
financial affairs, to which they contributed by working in the
departments of tobacco monopoly, public debt administration,
customs, and in the branch of the Agricultural Bank. We notice that
the municipal doctors of the central 'sancak' Şebinkarahisar were
often Greek. The Greeks in these offices did not usually number
more than one to each, and they were not in permanent employment.

After the Reforms, the Greeks were used by the Ottoman Government
to patronize the Christian population. They were given higher

positions in the political administration as assistants to the
'vali' and to the governors of the other 'sancaks' and some of
'kazas'.

A GENERAL VIEW OF ARMENIAN PARTICIPATION IN SIVAS

The participation of the Armenian community in public life of Sivas
was larger in the centres of the 'sancaks', especially in the
'sancak' of Sivas. The principal fields where the Armenian participation was really influential, were the departments of political
administration (administrative and municipal councils), of finance,
of justice and the secretariat. In the political and judicial
councils the Armenians were mere members, and they were not given
high positions, even after the Reforms of 1896. In financial
affairs the Armenians were the leading and predominant officials who
worked as managers, members, consultants, cashiers and clerks.
Members of the Armenian community also co-operated with the government of Sivas in the spheres of agriculture, public health and education. In the police force their part was kept to a minimum, but
in technical affairs they were treated well. From 1875/6 on, the
manager of the newly established press was an Armenian, namely
Andranik Efendi Vardanian.

SOME NOTABLE ARMENIANS IN THE PUBLIC LIFE OF SIVAS

ANSURIAN, Manuk. Born about 1863, 'for many years' he worked in the
postal and telegraphic service in Sivas. Then he became the
translator of the local French consulate.
ASLAN, Oskan. Born about 1853, he studied at Istanbul and in
Europe. He was a forest and mining inspector in Sivas.
BALIOZIAN, Ara. Born about 1865, the son of Petros, 'for many
years' he was a superintendent of police in the town of Sivas.
BOGHOSIAN, Baroyr (?-1911). He was a cashier in the taxation
department at Sivas.
DAGHAVARIAN, Dr Nazareth (1862-1915). Born in Sivas, he studied at
Istanbul and in France, at the Universities of Merchine and the
Sorbonne. In 1893, after graduating and getting diplomas and
degrees in agricultural engineering and medicine, he returned to
Istanbul and settled in Pera (Beyoglu) to practise medicine. In
1908 he was elected a deputy for Sivas in the Ottoman Parliament at
Istanbul.
DEVEDJIAN, Karekin (Garegin) Efendi (1868-12 January 1964). Born at
Harput, he studied in Istanbul, and then worked in the public debt
departments of Sivas, Bursa, Salonica and Beirut. From 1903 to 1908
he was a clerk in the public debt administration in the town of
Sivas. He has published a book in Turkish and French, 'Pêche et
pêcherie en Turquie', which has been highly appreciated.
FRENGÜLIAN, Yovhannes. He was a municipal architect in Sivas, in
the second half of the nineteenth century.
GABRIELIAN, Martiros Efendi (fl. in the second half of the nineteenth century). Originally from Muş, he became a provincial
translator in Sivas. He was succeeded by Seneqerim Kürkdjian who

embraced Islam, probably to retain his office permanently, but in spite of this the Turks did not spare his life in the massacres of the First World War.

GHUKASIAN, Kasbar. Originally from Cüngüş (Diyarbakir), he lived at Şebinkarahisar during the second half of the nineteenth century. Although uneducated, he was a clever merchant and a notable member of the Armenian community. Before the First World War, 'in the times of peace' he was elected a member to the local administrative council.

KALPAKLIAN, Dr Avedis (1872-c. 1935). Born in Maraş, he studied at the Imperial Military School of Medicine in Istanbul. In 1898, after graduating, he was sent to Zile (in Tokat) as a municipal doctor, where he served for four years. Then he moved to Gürün and worked there, again as a municipal doctor. In 1905 he returned home, to Maraş, and was employed there by the government as a teacher of physics in the secondary school. During the First World War he worked in the Ottoman army. For his services he was honoured by the Sublime Porte.

MESROPIAN, Karapet (fl. in the second half of the nineteenth century). He was a teacher in the government secondary school of Tokat.

MICHAYEL Efendi. From 1907 to 1908 he assisted the governor of Tokat. A. Alboyadjian, who has studied the history of the Armenians of Tokat, reflects on him and his predecessor (Yakob Tingirian) as follows:

Both of them were insignificant and uninfluential people who did not play any important role. Even the Armenians of Tokat have neglected their existence, and remember nothing about them.

MICHAYEL Efendi. He was a clerk in the public debt administration at the town of Sivas from 1903 to 1908.

NAZARETH Efendi. From 1900 to 1906 he assisted the governor of the 'sancak' of Amasya.

PARSEGHIAN, Sarkis. A learned and active man. According to our sources, 'he was the only chemist' at Şebinkarahisar.

PASBANIAN, Kevork (?-1915). Until 1912 he worked as a clerk in the chamber of archives.

PASCAL Efendi. He was the assistant to the deputy-governor of the 'kaza' of Gürün from about 1903 to 1908.

PASHAYAN, Dr Karapet (1864-1915). Born in Istanbul, he studied at the Imperial Military School. After graduating in 1888, he worked as a municipal doctor first (for a year), in Palu and Malatya, and then from January 1889 to August 1890 in Divrigi. In 1891-2 he practised his profession in Şebinkarahisar. He was beloved by both the Christians and Muslims.

SEFERIAN, Yakob. Before 1890 he officiated in the administration of justice in Tokat as 'juge d'instruction'.

SHAHINIAN, Yakob. In 1876 he was elected a deputy for Sivas in the Parliament of Istanbul.

SHIRINIAN, Kevork (1828-99). Born in Sivas, he studied medicine under Dr Henry West, and obtained permission from Istanbul to practise his profession. He settled in Tokat and 'for many years' worked as a municipal doctor there.

TCHERASUNIAN, Avedis (fl. in the second half of the nineteenth century). A landowner and merchant in Tokat, he acted as a judge in the local court of first instance.

TINGIRIAN, Yakob (1839-1909). Born at Istanbul and educated in London, from 1900 to 1903 he was the assistant to the governor of Tokat.

VEZNEYAN, Dr Yaruthiwn (1883-1915). Born in the Hüseynik village of Elâzig, he studied in the Imperial Military School of Medicine in Istanbul. In 1907, after graduating, he was sent to Talas and Zile in Tokat as a municipal doctor.

Chapter 7

THE ARMENIANS OF SEYHAN

HISTORICAL SURVEY

Seyhan is the new name of the province of Adana which in the second
half of the nineteenth century included the larger part of Cilicia.
The name Adana (Arb. Adana, Adâna, and later Atana; Arm. Atana, and
Ott.Turk. Âtana and Âdana) is explained by a Greek mythological
story according to which the brothers Adanus and Sarus built Adana
giving it their names; but in fact it is derived from the Hittite
'Ataniya', 'Adana'. (1) In the seventh century, at the time of the
Caliph Umar b. al-Khattâb, the Arabs came to Adana and occupied it.
The Byzantines kept up the fight for it and eventually conquered it
in the tenth century. In the eleventh century it fell to the Seljuk
rule.

Armenians are mentioned in Adana as early as the fourth century
AD, but by the beginning of the eleventh century they had much in-
creased in number, because Armenia had lost its independence and was
suffering from the harshness of the Seljuks. After the battle of
Malazgirt (26 August 1071) Philaretos, an Armenian commander in the
Byzantine army, withdrew to Cilicia and settled there, choosing
Maraş as his seat. (2) In 1080 when Dânishmend oppressed
Cappadocia, the Armenian vassal princes moved to Maraş and there
they received districts and strongholds from Philaretos as fiefs.
Ruben, one of these princes, gathered around him many supporters and
established a principality from 1080 to 1095. He was succeeded by
his son Kostandin, who extended the boundaries of his dominion with
new regions and castles. At that time when the Crusaders appeared,
the Armenians achieved good friendship and collaborated with them.
Adana at first in 1132 temporarily, but finally in 1172-3, was in-
corporated in the Armenian kingdom. In 1198, Levon, one of the
successors of Kostandin, was recognized as the vassal king of
Cilicia by the Emperor of Germany, Henry VI, by Alexis III of
Byzantium, and the Pope Celestine III of Rome. He organized his
court and army in a European form, and stimulated the arts and
trades. Levon's daughter Zabel married Hethum, the son of her
tutelar. They ruled together over Armenian Cilicia, Zabel until
1252, and her husband alone until 1270 when Hethum went to Karakorum
in 1254 and presented himself as a vassal king to the Mongol Great

Khan Möngke. (3) The Armenian and Mongol allied armies invaded
Syria and conquered Aleppo, Urfa and Damascus in 1260. On the death
of Möngke the victorious troops withdrew. Hethum's son, Levon III,
was attacked by the Egyptians in Tarsus, but he succeeded in
strengthening his army and together with the Mongols marched into
Syria as far as Hims. The dissolution of the Crusades and the
weakening of the Mongols left the Armenians of Cilicia alone to the
continual and violent offensive operations of the Mamelukes. The
last king, Levon VI, was captured in Sis on 16 April 1375 and taken
to Egypt. Later, being saved by ransom, he wandered through Europe
trying to rally support to regain his throne but did not succeed.
Thus the Armenian state of Cilicia came to its end. (4)

On the fall of the Armenian kingdom Adana with the surrounding
country passed to the Mamelukes. In 1378 its governor was the
Turkoman Yüregir-oglu Ramazân under the suzerainty of Egypt. The
Ramazân-oglu dominated there for more than two centuries. In 1608
it became a directly governed Ottoman 'eyalet'. From 1833 to 1840
Adana, together with Syria, was occupied by the Egyptians but was
subsequently ceded again to the Ottomans.

ADMINISTRATIVE STRUCTURE

In the second half of the nineteenth century, the province of Seyhan
(Adana) contained four 'sancaks': Seyhan (Adana), Içel, Kozan, and
Cebel-i Bereket. In 1305H/1887-8 the 'kaza' of Mersin in Seyhan was
transformed into a separate 'sancak' which included the 'kaza' of
Tarsus (formerly a part of the 'sancak' of Seyhan). The following
are the 'kazas' of the five 'sancaks'.
The 'kazas' of the 'sancak' of Seyhan:
 Adana
 Karaisali
 Ceyhan (Hamidiye)
  The 'kaza' of Ceyhan was added to Seyhan after the detachment
  of Mersin and Tarsus.
The 'sancak' of Mersin had the 'kaza' of Tarsus.
The 'kazas' of the 'sancak' of Içel:
 Silifke
 Ermenâk
 Mut
 Gülnar
 Anamur
The 'kazas' of the 'sancak' of Kozan:
 Kozan (Sis)
 Kadirli (Kars)
 Saimbeyli (Haçin)
 Feke
The 'kazas' of the 'sancak' of Cebel-i Bereket ('Cebel-i Bereket'
now is called ' Osmaniye', but I kept the old name in order not to
confuse it with the 'kaza' of Osmaniye):
 Yarpuz
 Osmaniye
 Islahiye
 Hassa

Bahçe (Bulanik)
Payas

POPULATION

The general population of this province in the second half of the
nineteenth century was, according to Cuinet, (5) about 403,500:
Armenians

Apostolic	69,300	
Catholic	11,550	
Protestant	16,600	
		97,450
Syrian Orthodox		20,900
Greek Orthodox		46,200
Latins and Maronites		4,539
Muslims		
Turk	93,200	
Kurd and Turkoman	39,600	
Circassian	13,200	
Syrian and Arab	12,000	
		158,000
Persians, Afghans and others		4,400
Gipsies		16,050
Fellahs, Ansaris and Nusayris		56,000
Total		403,539

Fraşerî in 1889 estimates the population of Adana as 350,000
Christians (the Armenians being the majority of them), Turks, Kurds,
and Arabs. (6) However, it is interesting to mention that the
number given by Cuinet for the Armenian inhabitants, viz. 97,450, is
exceptionally more than the figures recorded by the Armenian
sources. Ormanian, (7) followed by Lepsius (8) and the almanac of
Theodik, (9) presents the Armenian population as the following:

Adana (including Mersin and Içel)		
Apostolic	35,000	
Catholic	2,000	
Protestant	900	
		37,900
The 'sancak' of Kozan		
Apostolic	9,000	
Protestant	500	
		9,500
The 'kaza' of Saimbeyli		
Apostolic	20,000	
Catholic	1,000	
Protestant	200	
		21,200
Payas and the surrounding 'kazas' of Cebel-i Bereket		11,000
Total		79,600

The difference between the Turkish and Armenian statistics is
caused, first, by the non-existence of an official or reliable

census in the Ottoman Empire and second, in this particular case, by
the fact that the Armenians did not intend to obtain any independence in Adana, and on the other hand the Turks were not concerned
about any separatist movement.

THE TRADES AND PROFESSIONS OF ARMENIANS

Some of the Armenian inhabitants of the province of Seyhan were
engaged in the cultivation of cereals and fruit and in cattle
breeding. Their popular occupations, however, were the trades,
crafts and professions. They were especially busy in commerce: in
the manufacture of cloth, towels, handkerchiefs, bags, carpets,
earthenware, and various silver adornments. They also laboured in
tanning of leather, dye-works and painting, tinning, saddlery and
stone-masonry. The Armenian traders and artisans were concentrated
in the towns, and thus they presented the main industrial element.
Speaking of the district of Seyhan Ephrikian wrote:
> The local crafts are mostly in the hands of the Armenians, like-
> wise the commerce. They are also engaged in agriculture, for
> which they have brought special implements from Europe. (10)
Many Armenians also specialized in different professions and arts,
such as medicine, law, engineering, the postal and telegraphic service, and architecture. They were trained in the high schools and
institutions of Tarsus, Antep, Istanbul, Beirut and Damascus.

CENTRES OF ARMENIAN PARTICIPATION

The Armenians took a comparatively large part in the public life of
the central 'sancak', and particularly in the headquarters of the
province. Outside the centres, the Armenian influence was considerable in Tarsus (Mersin), in the 'kazas' Saimbeyli and Feke of
the 'sancak' Kozan, in Anamur (Içel), and Payas (Cebel-i Bereket).
It is worth noting that in Saimbeyli Armenian officials enjoyed
predominant positions and high rank.

MAIN FIELDS OF ARMENIAN PARTICIPATION

The participation of the Armenian community in the life of Seyhan
was largest in the centre of the province. At the headquarters
there were two or three Armenians on the administrative council re-
presenting the Apostolic, Catholic and Protestant communities. In
the rest of the 'vilâyet' one or two Armenians were elected to the
administrative councils. In the 'kazas' of Yarpuz and of Kozan
(Sis), which once was the seat of the Armenian kingdom, and until
the First World War was the see of the Armenian Patriarchate, there
were generally two Armenian members. From three to six Armenians
were elected to the municipality of Adana, while the other municipal
councils had only one or two Armenian members. It is remarkable
that the municipality of Saimbeyli was almost entirely left in the
hands of the Armenians.
    In the financial affairs, especially at Adana and Saimbeyli, the

Armenians took an important part. One to three were employed in the
control of revenue and expenditure and in the taxation department;
one or two in the Ottoman Bank, and between two and four in the
branch of the Agricultural Bank, as well as in the public debt and
in the salt administration. Their service was considerable also in
the tobacco monopoly where we find two or three of them. The
tobacco departments were sometimes entirely run by Armenian
officials.

As to the judicature, the Armenians were included in the courts
of first instance and of appeal at the headquarters. In each
division of the courts, i.e. civil and criminal, there was at least
one Armenian but in the criminal department of appeal there were
often two Armenian judges. Their influence was strongest in the
court of commerce where from three to five of them were to be found.
They also worked as executive officials, members of trial councils
and as notaries. In the outlying 'kazas' Armenians served the
courts of first instance and of commerce, and the executive departments. In the courts of central 'sancaks' they participated in both
offices of the judicial court, but in the courts of the outer
'kazas' only in the department of first instance, which had no
division into civil and criminal offices.

In the technical field, Armenians filled the posts of chief and
second engineers in the engineering department at Adana, and two or
three of them were foremen as well. In the public works there were
usually two, and in the post office at the section of foreign languages the directors and operators of the telegraphic service were
frequently Armenian. There were Armenian technicians in printing.
A compositor for Armenian is mentioned which implies that the press
also had a section for Armenian printing. At the railway stations
of Adana, Mersin and Tarsus about twenty Armenians worked as station
masters, mechanics and locomotive drivers. Outside the centre of
the 'vilâyet', the technical activity of the Armenians was limited
to the sphere of the postal and telegraphic service, and the public
works. As to the secretariat Armenians often held the positions of
clerk, accountant, and cashier in the various departments of the
local government. They were principally employed in the departments
of the chief secretariats, land registries, archives, customs, and
control of revenue. They were particularly many in the central
'sancaks', but were fewer in the outlying 'kazas'. In the latter
Armenian clerks worked mainly in the offices of chief secretariat,
land registry and customs. It is worth noting that many 'vilâyet'
translators were Armenian, of whom we can record the names of Tiran
and Avedis Efendis.

OTHER FIELDS OF ARMENIAN PARTICIPATION

Other fields of Armenian participation were agriculture, public
health, education and the police force. At Adana Armenian officials
filled posts on the forestry board, agricultural inspectorate, and
the board of trade, and in crafts and agriculture, there being about
two or three in each. They were also employed in the other central
'sancaks', but in the outer 'kazas' we scarcely ever find an
Armenian since there were often no special departments of

agriculture. In respect of education from two to four Armenians were included on the education council and committees, as cashiers or members, and a few taught in the preparatory, secondary and girls' schools. The 'salname' of 1319H/1901-2 mentions a teacher of the Armenian language in the secondary school of Adana, which attests to the fact that Armenian was taught there. I could not, however, check up from other sources how long Armenian was taught in that school. In the school of crafts as well, some Armenian masters taught shoe-making, tailoring and cabinet-making. In the police force at the headquarters of the province, Armenians were sometimes employed as assistant superintendents of police, police sergeants and policemen. There were no Armenian officials in the service of education and police, outside the city of Adana.

In the public health service, at the centres of the 'sancaks', Armenians held the position of doctor and chemist for the muni- cipalities, and in Adana they were also employed in the infirmary and army medical corps.

A GENERAL VIEW OF ARMENIAN PARTICIPATION IN SEYHAN

To summarize, the Armenian participation in public life of Seyhan was extended over political and financial administration, judicature and mechanical crafts. In these fields the part of Armenians was strong and steady. In the spheres of agriculture, the public health service and education, their contribution was limited, while in the police force very few Armenians were included.

It is interesting to note that in the 'kaza' of Saimbeyli (Haçin), the Armenian inhabitants of which were endowed with a courageous and freedom-loving spirit, Armenian participation in public life was larger and more regular. It seems ludicrous, but it would appear that the Turks, in organizing the public life of Saimbeyli, had taken into consideration the resisting disposition of the Armenians there.

SOME NOTABLE ARMENIANS IN THE PUBLIC LIFE OF SEYHAN

AGHA-SARKISIAN, Michayel Efendi (1857-1942). Born in Kozan (Sis), he became proficient at Turkish and served the local government in many ways and for many years. He was a member of the court of jus- tice first, and then the 'juge d'instruction'. He was also the clerk of the land registry office for a while. Later, until 1915, he was a member of the court of Osmaniye. In 1921 he settled in Beirut.

BABAHEKIAN, Thoros (1860-1917). Born in Saimbeyli, he learned carpentry and taught himself local constructional methods. He was employed by the municipality as engineer and architect, and his work and opinions were much appreciated. Many buildings in Saimbeyli were constructed under his management.

EVIKHANIAN, Karapet Efendi (1885-1919). For many years he worked in the telegraphic service of Saimbeyli, first as an ordinary official, and then as director.

FERMANIAN, Karapet Efendi (1847-1908?). Born in Kozan and the son

of Şahin, 'for many years' he was the cashier of the local public
finance administration. Archbishop Khad Atchapahian, an elder
from the Armenian Patriarchate of Sis, wrote in a private letter
(dated 5 March 1959, Damascus) the following about him:
> Karapet Efendi Fermanian was an influential Armenian. His
> dealings with other people revealed him as a diplomatic and
> understanding man who was very much beloved in government
> circles.

FERMANIAN, Şahin (1790-1876). Born in Kozan, from 1865 to 1876 he
participated as a member in the local municipal council and the
court of first instance.

KARAPET Efendi (fl.c. 1900). He was the manager of the branch of
the Ottoman Bank in Mersin.

KASPARIAN, Aristakes Efendi (1861-?). Born in Adana, between 1880
and 1882 he was an official in the foreign languages section of the
local telegraphic service. From 1883 to 1886 he was elected a
member to the court of first instance in Adana. From 1889 to 1891
he worked in the public debt administration as first clerk and consultant in legal matters. In 1908 he was elected a deputy for Adana
in the Ottoman Parliament of Istanbul.

KEVORKIAN (Satchlian), Andreas (1864-1938). Born in Kozan, he
studied in a Turkish school and in 1898 was licensed as a lawyer by
the government. He practised his profession and at the same time he
was a 'judicial' official.

KIRKYASHARIAN, Parsegh (1872-1920?). He studied in Saimbeyli and
Istanbul, and for a while was engaged in commerce. Later, 'for
many years' he served as a cashier in the public finance administration at Saimbeyli.

KÖR-AVEDIKIAN, Krikor Efendi (1841-1916). A member of the Armenian
Protestant community in Kozan, he practised for thirty years as a
lawyer, and was a government official as well for an unknown period.

KUYUMCIAN, Meguerditch (1875-1936). Born in Kozan, he studied first
in a local Armenian school and then in Istanbul in the Armenian
secondary School of Berberian. He worked in the administration of
tobacco monopoly in Kozan as assistant-manager and accountant.

MAMALIAN, Dr Sedrak (1875-c. 1940?). Born in Osmaniye, in 1899 he
went to Beirut to study medicine at the American University. In
1903, after graduating and getting his MD degree, he came to Adana
and worked there as a municipal doctor until 1909.

NALBANDIAN, Karapet Efendi (1873-c. 1950). Born in Kozan, he was a
wealthy landowner. He became proficient at Turkish and served in
the local government as a member of the administrative council and
the court of first instance, and as mayor.

NALBANDIAN, Mattheos Efendi (1876-1942). Originally from Kozan, in
1906 he became the deputy-governor of the 'kaza' of Saimbeyli, and
by his wise conduct satisfied both the government and the Armenian
community therein. In 1914 he was elected a deputy for Kozan in
the Ottoman Parliament at Istanbul.

NALBANDIAN, Yakob (1830-1907). Born in Kozan, he was a wealthy
landowner. Starting as a young man, he participated in the local
administrative council 'for many years'.

PASHABEZIAN, Krikor (1871-?). Born in Kozan, he studied in Adana
and Istanbul. In 1890, returning home, he was included in the court
of first instance, until the First World War.

PATATIAN, Karapet (1865-1934). He was a member of the administrative council and of the court of first instance in Kozan.
RECEBIAN, Hambartzum (1845-1918). Born in Saimbeyli, he was first a
merchant, but then served the Ottoman Government. According to our
source, 'for many years' (starting in 1896?) he was a consultant to
the local deputy-governor, and for three years the mayor. For his
services he was given decoration from the Sublime Porte.
SEKSENIAN, Martiros (1858-?). Born in Saimbeyli, the son of the
mayor Minas, he served the government for many years. He worked as
a cashier in the administration of public finance, and as a clerk in
the chief secretariat, in the census office and in the land
registry. In 1923 he settled in Beirut.
SEKSENIAN, Minas. Born in Saimbeyli, he was the mayor of the town
from 1879 to 1894. During his office Saimbeyli greatly flourished
with new buildings, roads, bridges and drains. He was succeeded by
other Armenian mayors, until the First World War, who were: Kevork
Mangerian, Hambartzum Recebian, Minas Bahadurian, Yaruthiwn
Shekherdemian and Karapet Keshishian.
SHEKHERDEMIAN, Karapet (1844-99). Born in Saimbeyli, he was engaged
in trading. In 1875 he was elected to 'the highest post in the
government' (deputy-governor?), and he was very helpful both to the
Christians and to the Muslims.
SISLIAN, Avedis Efendi. From 1903 to 1908 he was the provincial
translator of Seyhan.
SOGHANALIAN, Avedik (1869-1920). Born in Saimbeyli, he became a
cloth merchant. He served the local government as cashier, and as a
member of the court of first instance and of the municipal council.
He was 'twice elected deputy' for Saimbeyli in the Ottoman Parliament at Istanbul.
TAKVORIAN, Boghos Efendi (1860-1909). He was a chief engineer in
Adana.
TERZIAN, Yaruthiwn (1858-1920). Born in Saimbeyli, after finishing
his studies, he entered government service. He became the cashier
of the local public finance administration and a member of the
municipal council. 'For more than fifteen years' he was a member of
the court of first instance, and for eighteen years a member of the
administrative council as well. Although he was condemned to forced
labour a few times, still for his public services was given
decorations from the Sublime Porte (Ottoman policy!).
TIRDATIAN, Haci (1877-1920). Born in Saimbeyli, the son of Simon,
he studied in a local Armenian school. 'For a while' he was the
cashier of the public finance administration in Feke. He rendered
many services to the government of Saimbeyli.
TOPALIAN, Sokrat. Originally from Saimbeyli, in 1896 he was the
municipal chemist of Kozan.
URFALIAN, David Efendi (1859-1909). Born in Adana, he served the
local government in many ways. He was a member of the court of
appeal.
ZAHREDJIAN, Stephan (?-1909). Being employed by the Ottoman public
debt administration, he was the sericultural inspector in Adana.

Chapter 8

THE ARMENIANS OF ELÂZIG

HISTORICAL SURVEY

The province of Elâzig (shortened form of Mamûret ül-Azîz) covered
the districts of Harput (Kharpût), Mezre, Malatya (Malâtiya) and
Hozat (Khozât). In the days of Sultan Abdül'aziz (1861-76) Mezre
became an important governmental and military centre, and was called
Mamûret ül-Azîz ('the town rendered prosperous by Azîz') by the
'vali' Ismâ'îl Paşa in honour of the Sultan. After the proclamation
of the 'vilâyet nizamnamesi' (province regulations), together with
Harput it formed a 'mutasarriflik', first attached to Diyarbakir and
then independent (1875), until 1296H/1878-9 when it was re-organized
as a separate province. (1)
    Harput (Greek Xarpote, Arb. Khartabirt, and Ott.Turk. Kharpût) is
explained by the Armenian form Kharberd (pronounced 'Kharpert') or
Qarberd. 'Berd' means 'castle', but the origin of the word 'khar'
is obscure. This could be either an old local name or the same as
the Armenian 'qar', i.e. stone. Anyhow, historically the district
of Harput corresponds to the province of Anzit or Hanzit (Greek
'Anzêtinîs, Xanzit, Syriac Anzît or Hanzît, and Arb. Hanzît or
Hinzît) in ancient Armenia, the castle of which is mentioned by his-
torians and geographers under the name Ziad or Ziata (Latin Ziata
castellum, Syriac Ziyât and Hisna de Zaid, Arb. Hisn Ziyâd, and Ott.
Turk. Hisn Ziyâd).
    In the twelfth century the Turkoman Artuqid house, and in the
thirteenth century the Ayyûbids and the Seljuks dominated Harput.
In 1230 it was occupied by the Mongols, but three years later (631H/
1233-4) the Seljuk Sultan Alâ' al-Dîn Kayqubâdh conquered it. The
history of the Seljukid period is confused and almost unknown. In
the middle of the fourteenth century Harput was governed by the
Turkoman tribes of Eretna and Dhû'l-Qâdir. In 767H/1365-6 the
Egyptians seized it, and towards the end of that century the monarch
of Sivas, Qâdi Ahmed Burhân al-Dîn took possession of it and
defended himself there against the Aq-Qoyûnlu Qara Osmân.
    The Mongol Emperor Tîmûr on his return from the campaign of
Anatolia, subjugated Harput also to his dominion. After Tîmûr the
tribe of Dhû'l-Qâdir ruled there again, and in the days of Melik
Arslân the Aq-Qoyûnlu Uzun Hasan occupied it. In 913H/1507-8 it

came under the rule of the Safawî Shâh Ismâ'îl, but the vizier of
the Sultan Selîm I, Biyikli Mehmed Paşa after the conquest of
Diyarbakir (921-3H/1515-17) brought Harput also under the immediate
government of the Sublime Porte.

ADMINISTRATIVE STRUCTURE

The 'vilâyet' of Elâzig contained three 'sancaks' and eighteen
'kazas' as follows.
The 'kazas' of the 'sancak' of Elâzig:
   Elâzig (Harput-Mezre)
   Arapkir
   Kemaliye (Egin)
   Keban (Kebân Ma'den)
The 'kazas' of the 'sancak' of Malatya:
   Malatya
   Besni (Behisni)
   Adiyaman (Hisni Mansur)
   Kâhta
   Akçadag
The 'kazas' of the 'sancak' of Hozat (Dersim):
   Hozat
   Çemişgezek
   Pültümür (Kuziçan)
   Peri (Çarsancak)
   Mazgirt
   Ovacik
   Pertek
   Pah
   Nazimiye (Kizil-Kilise)

POPULATION

The provincial year-book of 1312H/1894-5 estimates the number of the
Armenian inhabitants as 75,416, (2) and adds 357 'stranger
Armenians'. Cuinet records the total population of Elâzig as about
575,314, of which 69,718 were Armenians, 650 Greeks, and the rest
were Turks, Kurds and Kizilbash. The same author gives the
following detailed statistics for the Armenian population: (3)

   'Sancak' of Elâzig
Apostolic	39,343	
Catholic	905	
Protestant	5,100	
		45,348

   'Sancak' of Malatya
Apostolic	15,080	
Catholic	770	
Protestant	350	
		16,200

'Sancak' of Hozat
Apostolic	7,560
Protestant	610
	8,170

Total   69,718

It will be noticed that once again Cuinet has been more conservative than the Turks. The numbers given by the Armenian sources for the Armenians of Elâzig are quite different from the above quoted estimations. Theodik's almanac presents the approximate total of the Armenians as 204,000, (4) while Ormanian, (5) followed by Lepsius, estimates it at about 131,200, thus:

Harput	51,000
Kemaliye	10,200
Arapkir	19,500
Çemişgezek	9,000
Peri	18,500
Malatya	23,000

We are inclined to accept Ormanian's statistics as, relatively speaking, more reliable.

TRADES AND PROFESSIONS OF ARMENIANS

The Armenians of the province of Elâzig were engaged in cultivation in the fields and on the mountains, and in the towns they were busy in various trades, crafts and professions. The compiler of the history of the Armenians in Elâzig attests the following concerning the economic situation of the Armenian community:

Many Armenians in Kharberd [Harput] were land owners. At the beginning of the last quarter of the last century, three-fourths of the land belonged to Turkish aghas, but by 1908, more and more Armenians became property owners. No doubt the money sent to their families by those who had emigrated to the United States, helped to bring about this change. In spite of government restrictions and blind hatred of Islam, the Armenians took advantage of any opportunity and it can be said without reservations that in the field of economics the Armenians became the more superior and the management of real estate passed into the hands of the Armenians, as also business, industry, arts and crafts due to the higher mentality of the Armenian and his ambition and vision. (6)

In Harput many Armenians were occupied in the textile industry, dealing with imports and exports. The brothers Fabrikatorian and Kürkdjian Krikor and the son Khosrov had big concerns manufacturing silk textiles. Other renowned firms in textiles were the families of Shaghalian, Hambartzumian, Tevrizian, Enovchian, Tüfenkdjian, Hindlian, Darakdjian, Demirdjian, etc. According to Ephrikian the handwork of the Armenian ladies, the works of fine goathair, and the beautifully woven rugs and carpets were appreciated very much. (7)

The Armenians co-operated with the Ottoman Government in mining and iron work also. At Maden (Ergani Madeni) the Ignatiosian family were engaged in copper mining, and at Keban the Arpiarian family worked the silver mines by Imperial writ. The iron factory of the

Parikian Brothers in Harput was well known and even carried out work
for the government. In his eye-witness account Nathanian states
that the Armenians made various 'European' arms, cartridges, and
'other machines'. (8)
    In the other 'kazas' also of the 'sancak' of Elâzig the Armenians
were the main industrial element. Almost all of the craftsmen of
Arapkir were Armenian, and in Kemaliye 'the majority of the merchants, of the retailers, chemists and watch-makers were Armenian...
but half of the carpenters and hair-dressers were Armenian, and the
other half were Turkish.' (9)
    In the 'sancak' of Malatya the Armenians were engaged in the pre-
paration of dried fruits, in cotton textiles and various crafts and
professions. Alboyadjian gives the following evidence:
    95 per cent of the artisans were Armenian. These by virtue of
    their crafts stayed economically secure. So the most vital and
    essential and as well lucrative arts were in the hands of the
    Armenians. Among the Turks also there were people more or less
    skilled in crafts, but their number was limited, as was the
    number of Armenian agriculturists. (10)
In the 'sancak' of Hozat (Dersim) both agriculture and industry were
backward, possibly because the majority of the population was
Kurdish. Only in the 'kazas' of Çemişgezek and Peri were the
Armenians occupied in the cultivation of cereals.
    In the province of Elâzig the popular professions of the
Armenians were medicine and pharmacy.

CENTRES OF ARMENIAN PARTICIPATION

The participation of the Armenian community in public life was
steady in the 'sancaks' of Elâzig and Malatya. In all 'kazas' of
these districts, except Akçadag (in Malatya), the Armenians had a
striking participation in different fields of the government
affairs.
    In Hozat (Dersim) the Armenians' service in public administration
was noteworthy only in the 'kazas' of Çemişgezek and Peri. In the
other parts of the 'sancak' also the Armenians worked for the
government, but their contribution was limited to a few departments
and was not strong, possibly because comparatively they were not so
many in number.

MAIN FIELDS OF ARMENIAN PARTICIPATION

At the headquarters of the province, in the administrative council
of Elâzig the Armenians had regularly four representatives: two
elected and two ex officio members, the latter being the spiritual
heads of the Apostolic and Catholic communities. In the 'kaza' of
Arapkir, in addition to the two elected Armenians, there were two or
three ex officio members, the third of whom was the controller of
revenue and expenditure (c. 1887-91). In 1880-1 even the parson of
the Armenian Protestant community took part there in the administrative council in virtue of his office. At Kemaliye the head of the
Apostolic community was alone an ex officio member, having beside

him one or two elected Armenian participants. In the 'kaza' of
Keban the Armenian representatives, one or two, were usually
elected, but from about 1890 to 1895, the Armenian clerk of the tax
collecting board was an ex officio member. At the centre of the
'sancak' of Malatya the Armenians had two elected members of the
administrative council, and after 1890 the prelates of the Apostolic
and Catholic communities were continuously appointed as ex officio
members. In the 'kazas' of Besni and Adiyaman, two, and at Kâhta and
Akçadag one or two, Armenians were usually elected to the council.
At the centre of the 'sancak' of Hozat and in the 'kazas' of
Çemişgezek and Peri there were normally two Armenian elected
members, but in Mazgirt, Ovacik and Nazimiye only one member would
be found, as elected or ex officio, the latter being the controller
of revenue.

At Elâzig from four to nine Armenians (in 1887-8 nine) were included on the municipal council of the provincial headquarters. In
the 'kazas' of the central 'sancak' there were usually two Armenians
elected to the council, but in Kemaliye they were sometimes three in
number. At Malatya two or three Armenians sat on the municipal
council; in Adiyaman and Besni after 1890 two members were given
posts, while in Kâhta and Akçadag there were no Armenians at all.
In the 'sancak' of Hozat, Armenian members were elected occasionally
to the municipal councils about 1880 and after 1900, but only in the
districts of Peri (Çarsancak), Çemişgezek and Mazgirt.

Out of the administrative and municipal councils, the Armenians
in the political administration of Elâzig served on the imputation
committee of the central headquarters and on the governing bodies of
some 'nahiyes'. After 1890, at Elâzig there were one or two
Armenians on the imputation committee which was formed within the
superintendence of the administrative council. In 1298H/1880-1 in
the central 'sancak' of the province eight Armenians were assistants
to the administrators of different 'nahiyes', and two others were
administrators. At the 'nahiye' of Argavan in Keban, from about
1887 to 1895, the taxation department and title-deed's clerks were
Armenian. In 1907-8 Armenians assisted the governing officials of
the 'nahiyes' of Agin, Iliç and Abuçeh in Kemaliye. One would
expect that after the Reforms of 1896 there would be Armenian assistants to the 'mutasarrifs' and to the 'kaymakams', but this is not
so. Only between c. 1900 and 1908 did an Armenian assist the
'vali', and for the 'kazas' of Arapkir and Peri Armenian assistant-
governors were appointed.

In the economic field of Elâzig many Armenians co-operated with
the Turks in various capacities. In the finance department the
cashier was normally Armenian, and apart from that there were always
about two clerks in the secretariat. In 1884-5 six and in 1907-8
three Armenian officials worked at the chamber of commerce, one or
two in the customs, and in the tax collecting board four Armenians
would be found. From 1880 to 1885 there were Armenian clerks and
cashiers in the tithe administration too. The Armenian participation was particularly large and steady in the 'régie' where the
cashier and the storekeeper were usually Armenian. Apart from them
two or three others also, acted as advocate, clerk and accountant.
It is interesting to note that in 1887-8 the head of the tobacco
monopoly was Armenian, and in 1894-5 nine Armenian officials were

employed there.   In public debt administration two or three
Armenians were included as clerks or inspectors.   In 1907-8 the
chief secretary and the memoranda clerk, as well as the silk inspector agent and the guard of this department were Armenian.   In the
'kazas' of the 'sancak' of Elâzig one or two Armenians worked in the
office of controller of revenue, and in the 'régie', the Agricultural Bank, and in the administration of public debt and of tithe
(1880-5).   At Keban between 1884 and 1891 and at Arapkir from 1884
to 1908 the sole administrators of tobacco monopoly were Armenian,
and in Kemaliye there was always an Armenian.   In the latter 'kaza'
between 1880 and 1885 the managers of public debt administration
were Armenian, and at Arapkir in 1907-8 a certain Mansurian Efendi
was the accountant and at the same time the clerk of that office.
At the centre of the 'sancak' of Malatya the public finance cashier
was always Armenian;   in 'régie' the chief agent or the clerk was
Armenian, and in public debt administration from 1884 to 1888 the
one and only official was Armenian.   Tax-collectors and members of
the chamber of agriculture and crafts were occasionally Armenian.
In the 'kazas' of Malatya the Armenians worked mostly in the control
of revenue, often as cashiers.   They were sometimes employed also in
the branch of the Agricultural Bank and in the administration of
tithes.   In the 'sancak' of Hozat, at Hozat, Peri and Çemişgezek the
Armenians co-operated with the government serving as tax-collectors,
as cashiers in public finance, and as agents or clerks in the
tobacco monopoly, but their participation was not regular.
      In judicature of the provincial headquarters at Elâzig there were
always two Armenian judges in the court of first instance, one in
the civil and another in the criminal section.   After 1890 two
Armenians sat also in the court of appeal.   Between 1880 and 1890
two or three Armenian members were included on the commercial court.
In 1884-5 the executive officer was Armenian.   Sometimes Armenian
clerks were employed in the court of first instance.   In the 'kazas'
of Elâzig an Armenian member was regularly elected to the court of
first instance, and from time to time other officials were employed
as well.   At Arapkir in 1887-8 the notary was Armenian, and between
1887 and 1895 the process servers were usually Armenian.   In
Kemaliye in 1887-8 the assistant of the 'juge d'instruction' and in
1890-1 the process server were Armenian.   At the centres of Malatya
and Hozat two Armenian judges participated in the court of first
instance, one in the civil and the other in the criminal division.
In the 'kazas' of these 'sancaks' where the court was not separated
into civil and criminal departments, an Armenian would always be
found in the court of first instance, but in Hozat this was true
only for Peri, Çemişgezek and Mazgirt.

OTHER FIELDS OF ARMENIAN PARTICIPATION

In the spheres of technical affairs, of the secretariat, education,
agriculture and public health the Armenian participation was noteworthy, but not so strong as in the other departments.   At Elâzig,
at the government headquarters, the technical contribution of
Armenians was limited to the engineering department.   The Armenians
worked there as first or second engineers and as foremen.   It is

interesting to mention that in 1894-5 the municipal engineer, and
two other engineers as well in the engineering department, were
Armenian. In the rest of the province the Armenian participation in
technical fields fluctuated. However, at Arapkir in 1890-1 two
Armenians were acting in the road building board, and at Hozat in
1889-90 the chief engineer was Armenian.

Apart from being in charge of records and accounts in different
government offices, the Armenians were employed as well in purely
secretarial departments. At Elâzig in the chief secretariat there
was usually an Armenian clerk. In 1880-1 and 1884-5 three Armenians
worked on the land registry, and in the postal and telegraphic service an Armenian clerk would be found. In the 'kazas' of Elâzig
there were occasionally from one to three Armenians in the land
registry, and curiously enough at Arapkir an Armenian clerk was
acting in the birth registry (census office), although not frequently. In Malatya only at the centre, and at Besni and in Hozat only
in the 'kaza' of Peri, Armenian officials worked from time to time
in the land registry.

In the field of education, the Armenians co-operated with the
local government as teachers and as members of the education committees. At the centre of the 'vilâyet' usually two or three
Armenians participated in the education council, while in the
'kazas' of Arapkir, Kemaliye and Keban one or two Armenians would
sometimes be found in the education committees as against two
Turkish members. At Elâzig itself in the government secondary
school Armenian teachers were occasionally employed. For instance,
Bedros (Petros) Efendi taught French and geography there c. 1887-90.
It is worthy of note that in the same school from about 1890 to 1908
the Armenian language was taught as in some other provinces. In the
rest of the province there was no Armenian participation in educational affairs.

At Elâzig in 1880-1 there were four Armenians in the agricultural
inspectorate, and in 1889-90 two members served on the trade and
agricultural board. At Arapkir in 1890-1 three Armenians were included on the trade and agricultural board. At the centre of the
province in 1890-1 the chemist and the vaccinator, and in 1894-5 the
chemist and the doctor of second municipality, were Armenian. In
the 'kaza' of Arapkir only in 1907-8 was the municipal physician
Armenian. As to the police force, in the year 1907 at Elâzig there
were two assistant superintendents of police and one policeman, but
in each station of Arapkir, Malatya, Adiyaman and Besni, one
Armenian policeman was included. At Keban in the same year two
policemen were employed.

COMPARATIVE NOTE: GREEK PARTICIPATION

The Greek participation in public life of the province of Elâzig was
very irregular. However, we find Greek officials in the departments
of political administration, finance, justice, technical affairs,
the secretariat and public health. Their activity was limited to
the central 'sancak' of Elâzig, but in Malatya in 1889-90 and 1894-5
the municipal doctors were Greek. As to their number, there was not
more than one in each department.

In political administration, at Keban in 1907-8 there was a Greek
member in the local council, and in Kemaliye in 1890-1 a Greek
member served on the administrative council. At the centre of the
province, in 1907-8 the judicial inspector was Greek, as was the
officer of the commercial court in Kemaliye (1907-8). Again at
Elâzig in the tobacco monopoly in 1890-1 and 1894-5 there were Greek
officials. A Greek worked in the Agricultural Bank in 1890-1 and in
1894-5 the assistant manager was Greek. At Arapkir in 1890-1 a certain Idris Efendi was the public finance agent, and at Kemaliye, in
1907-8, in tobacco monopoly, and in 1890-1 in the Agricultural Bank
one Greek would be found.
     In the secretariat, at the centre of the province in 1880-1 there
was a Greek registrar, as was another Greek in the chief secretariat
in 1884-5. In 1887-8 and 1889-90 Greek officials were employed in
the chamber of archives, but in 1894-5 and 1907-8 the managers of
the same chamber were Greek. In the field of technical affairs, in
1889-90, the chief engineer of Elâzig was Greek, and in 1890-1 the
assistant administrator of the provincial press was Greek as well.

A GENERAL VIEW OF ARMENIAN PARTICIPATION IN ELÂZIG

The Armenian participation in public life of the 'vilâyet' of Elâzig
was largest in the central 'sancak', i.e. in the provincial headquarters and in the 'kazas' of Arapkir, Kemaliye and Keban. The
spheres of strong Armenian influence were the political administration, finance and justice. In technical affairs, the secretariat,
education, agriculture, and the public health service also, the
Armenians took part, but their activity was not consistent in these
fields. As in the other provinces, in Elâzig too the Armenians were
intentionally kept out of the police force, so that they could not
exercise this power in any way.
     It is of special interest that the Armenian language was taught
in the government secondary school at Elâzig; the teachers were
Yovhannes Efendi Yazidjian and Eduard Efendi.

SOME NOTABLE ARMENIANS IN THE PUBLIC LIFE OF ELÂZIG

ARDZRUNI, Nishan (1849-95). Born in the village of Abuçeh
(Kemaliye), he studied in the Medical Military School at Istanbul.
In 1871 having graduated, he entered the service of the Ottoman army
as a chemist and surgeon. From 1881 to 1889 he was employed as
municipal doctor in the 'kazas' of Kemaliye and Çemişgezek.
ARSLAN, Dr Eduard. Studied medicine at the University of Padua and
graduated in 1889. About 1890 he was appointed as municipal doctor
in Elâzig.
ASASIAN, Yovhannes Efendi. He was the assistant to the 'vali' of
Elâzig from about 1900 to 1908.
BEGIAN, Kevork (1848-94). He studied medicine at the Medical Mili-
tary School of Istanbul and, returning home, served the government.
He was employed as municipal doctor in Harput, Arapkir, Kemaliye,
Bitlis and Erzurum.
BULUTIAN, Abgar (fl. in the second half of the nineteenth century).

He was a member of the administrative council of Peri.

DER-DAVIDIAN, Sarkis (c. 1860-1935). A learned man and a merchant, he served the court of Malatya (c. 1890) as a member of the public prosecution board. From 1895 to 1897 he lived in Elâzig and in 1907 he went to settle in America with his family.

DJELDJELIAN, Yaruthiwn (1870-1915). Born and educated at Malatya, he taught French in the local government secondary school. At the same time he also taught French and Turkish in the Latin school of Malatya.

DZERON, Manuk (1862-1938). Born in the village of Perçenç (Elâzig) and educated in the Euphrates College of Harput, he studied civil engineering at the University of Istanbul. On his return home, in 1886, he was employed as assistant to the provincial engineer. For about four years he co-operated in the road building works. Not tolerating the oppression of the rulers, in 1890 he emigrated to the USA.

ENSHERIAN, E. (1846-1910). Originally from Diyarbakir he studied medicine in New York and graduated in 1877. Returning home, he worked as municipal doctor first in Elâzig for about ten years, and then in Trebizond for seven years. After the troubles of 1895, he settled in America.

ERMOYAN, Yaruthiwn. He was a tax collector in the 'kaza' of Peri.

HELVADJIAN, Artin (c. 1850-1915). He studied medicine at the Medical Military School of Istanbul, and for 'forty long years served the Turkish government' at Elâzig. For his conscientious services he was given decorations by the Sublime Porte.

HOLOBIKIAN, Krikor. A leader of the Armenian Protestant community at Peri, he was educated in the Euphrates College of Harput. He served the local government of Peri as mayor.

IGNATIOSIAN, Boghos (1837-1905). Born in the village of Hüseýnik (Elâzig), he was engaged in sericulture. He supplied the Turkish army in Elâzig with clothes. In 1876 he settled in Ergani Madeni and was employed in the mining administration. At the same time he imported sewing machines from Europe. In 1893 he returned to Harput.

KALINIAN (Terzian), Khoren. In 1899 he graduated from the Euphrates College of Harput and taught for one year in the Protestant School of Malatya. Then he went to study medicine in the American University of Beirut, and soon after finishing his course he became municipal doctor of Mezre for three years. According to our source, later 'for ten years' he served in the army medical corps and afterwards went to Egypt and settled in Alexandria.

KESHISHIAN, Michayel (1874-1943). Studying medicine, he graduated in 1898 from the American University of Beirut and the next year received a diploma from the Medical Military School of Istanbul. After 1902 he officiated as a municipal and court doctor in Malatya.

KETCHIAN, Araqel (1885-?). Born in Kemaliye, he studied at the Aramean School of the village of Gemirgâp. After finishing his course he served in the finance administration in Kemaliye as accountant, until 1908. Then he settled in Istanbul where he continued to work as government official.

KÜNDÜBEGIAN, Serob Efendi (c. 1868-1915). In 1893 he became the manager of land registry and also an agent in public finance administration at Malatya. In 1904 he was superintendent of police in the 'kaza' of Adiyaman (Hisni Mansur).

KÜNDÜBEGIAN, Yovhannes (c. 1865-1915). From 1890 to 1903 he was an agent for the taxation department and a member of the judicial court in Malatya.

MAKARIAN, Makar (?-1915). A learned man who served his community and the government. He was the administrator of the village of Kuyulu (Elâzig) where he was born. He founded the local Armenian Lusavortchakan school.

MISSAKIAN, Marka Efendi (fl. in the second half of the nineteenth century). For 'many years' he was a municipal engineer at Elâzig and Erzurum.

TCHUGASIZIAN, Minas Efendi. He was the assistant to the deputy-governor of the 'kaza' of Peri from about 1903 to 1908.

TCHUGASIZIAN, Sarim. He was the assistant to the deputy-governor of the 'kaza' of Arapkir from about 1905 to 1908.

TERKHANIAN, Michayel Efendi (1865-1915). From about 1880 to 1909 he served the government of Malatya in various offices. First he was employed as an agent in the tax collection, but then was assigned cashier to the 'kaza' of Adiyaman. In 1889 returning to Malatya he continued to work in finance administration as cashier (until 1909). According to our source, he was also a member of the administrative and municipal councils, and of the court of justice.

TIWTELIAN, Yovhannes (1855-1895). Educated at Malatya and Istanbul he served the government of Malatya. From 1873 to 1888 he was the first clerk in the chief secretariat and between 1888 and 1895 he officiated as the cashier of the public finance administration.

TOTVAYAN, Boghos. In 1895 he was appointed assistant to the deputy-governor of the 'kaza' of Peri (Çarsancak), but he was killed by the brigands of Arslân Bey.

YAGHDJIAN, Ohan (c. 1800-c. 1890). He lived in Kesirik (Elâzig) and was a merchant. During the Russo-Turkish War he supplied the Ottoman army with food, working under difficult conditions. For his services he was offered decorations and an honorary dress with a sword.

YAZIDJIAN, Yovhannes Efendi (fl. in the second half of the nineteenth century). He was a provincial dragoman, and a teacher of Armenian in the government secondary school at Elâzig.

Chapter 9

THE ARMENIANS OF SYRIA
I. THE PROVINCE OF ALEPPO

HISTORICAL SURVEY

Aleppo is an old Assyrian city which is mentioned in the historical records of Boghazköy under the name Hallap (Hallaw or Halvan), as early as the second millennium BC. The Hittite king Mursilis I (1620-1590 BC) destroyed Aleppo and took its treasures and slaves to his capital Hattusa. It was then dominated by the Medes but in about 1430 BC it passed again to the Hittites.

In 312 BC Seleucus Nikator, a commander of Alexander the Great, founded the Seleucid dynasty in Syria. He renamed Aleppo 'Beroia' and established a Macedonian colony there. In 64 BC it became part of the Roman province of Syria and during the Byzantine period it was devastated, together with Antioch, by the Persians in 540. The Emperor Justinian rebuilt the town and erected a beautiful cathedral there.

In 16H/637 Aleppo was conquered by the Arab Muslims under the command of Khalîd ibn al-Wâlid. Although the Seljuk Turks had remained there since the days of Mirdâsîs (eleventh century), it came under direct Ottoman government in the sixteenth century.

The association of Armenians with Aleppo goes back as far as the first century BC (84-83 BC) when Tigran the Great annexed Syria and Lebanon to his empire and for fourteen years Syria was governed by the Armenian armies. From the third to the sixth century the Roman emperors established military colonies in Syria and on the mountains of Lebanon of the Armenian warrior satrapies. About AD 632-40 there were Armenian soldiers serving the Byzantine and Sassanid armies in Syria against the Arabs. After 1045, on the fall of Ani, the capital of Armenia, many Armenians were pushed towards Cilicia and Syria. There were apparently several organized Armenian communities in Syria in the twelfth century, because when the Catholicos Krikor (Grigor) IV assembled a church-council in Rumkale (Halfeti) in 1179, six Armenian bishops took part in it who came from Mesopotamia and Syria. These were Bishop Kevork of Miyafarkin (Silvan), Archbishop Stephanos of Urfa, Archbishop Grigorios of Antioch, Bishop Kostandin of Apamea, Bishop Sarkis (Sargis) of Lâdhikiyya, and Archbishop Sahak of Jerusalem.

In the eleventh to fourteenth centuries, at the time of the

Armenian kingship of Cilicia, there were Armenian communities
flourishing in the main towns of Syria: Aleppo, Hamah, Lâdhikiyya,
Antioch, and Damascus. After the fall of Cilicia, the Armenians
moved more and more into Syria for safety. In the fourteenth century Aleppo especially became a centre for Armenians, where they had
their church, school and community leaders, both clerical and lay.
A Gospel written in 1355 by Yovhannes, son of the priest Lazar, was
acquired in 1379 by an Armenian 'Âmir' in Aleppo. (1) In 1400 the
head of the Armenian community was a certain Tawakal, son of
Karapet. (2) In 1499-1500 the church of Forty Martyrs in the
quarter of Salibah was enlarged at the expense of Reis Isa. After
this renovation Aleppo became next to Sis (Kozan), the second seat
of the Catholicate of Cilicia, where the patriarchs resided from
time to time. From the beginning of the sixteenth century the
Armenian community of Aleppo had its regular episcopal prelacy,
archbishop Khatchadur (c. 1525-45) being the first prelate of this
new period. About the bishops of Aleppo before Khatchadur we know
very little. Only two bishops are mentioned in history books:
Bishop Yovhannes who in 1307 took part in the church-council of Sis;
and Bishop Yovakim who in 1438 participated in the council of
Florence.

During the sixteenth and seventeenth centuries many new Armenians
came from Julfa (Old Julfa in Armenia) to settle in Aleppo. These
people were talented merchants and contributed much to the community
life and trade of the city. Until 1915-20, however, the Armenians
of Aleppo were not numerous. After the massacres of the First World
War thousands of Armenians fled from Anatolia into Syria and sought
refuge in the different towns of Syria and especially in Aleppo.
There are now about 100,000 Armenians in the Syrian Arab Republic.

ADMINISTRATIVE STRUCTURE

In the nineteenth century, under the Ottoman dominion, Syria was
divided into three parts:
  (a) 'Vilâyet' of Aleppo
  (b) 'Vilâyet' of al-Shâm, and,
  (c) 'Mutasarriflik' of Dayr al-Zor.
  The 'mutasarriflik' (an independent 'sancak') of Dayr al-Zor was
a separate administrative unit; the province of Shâm included parts
of Lebanon, whereas the 'vilâyet' of Beirut had the 'sancak' of
Lâdhikiyya in it. It is quite evident that until 1 September 1920,
when General Henrie-Joseph-Eugène Gouraud, the High Commissioner of
France, proclaimed the creation of the Lebanese State ('État du
Grand Liban'), Lebanon was included in the title 'Syria'. This is
why it has been taken in the present work.
  The province of Aleppo contained three 'sancaks': Aleppo, Maraş
and Urfa, which were divided into twenty-three 'kazas' as follows.
The 'kazas' of the 'sancak' of Aleppo:
    Aleppo (Halab)
    Gaziantep (Antep)
    Kilis
    Iskenderun
    Antakya (Antioch)

Belen (Beylan)
Jabal Sam'ân
Hârem
Idleb
Jisr al-Shughûr
Ma'arrat ul-Nu'mân
al-Bâb-Jabbûl
Manbij
al-Rakkah
The 'kazas' of the 'sancak' of Maraş:
Maraş
Süleymanli (Zeytun)
Elbistan
Pazarcik
Andirin
The 'kazas' of the 'sancak' of Urfa:
Urfa
Birecik
Halfeti (Rumkale)
Suruç
The 'mutasarriflik' of Dayr al-Zor had four 'kazas' as follows:
Dayr al-Zor
al-Ashârah
Ra's ul-'Ayn
Abu Kamâl

POPULATION

Owing to the lack of an official census there are no complete and
reliable statistics for the Armenian population of the province of
Aleppo. The figures of Cuinet are so spread over the general
statistics of the different towns and 'sancaks' of the 'vilâyet',
that it is impossible to collect them and present his total for the
Armenians of Aleppo. The provincial year-book of 1908 gives the
following (3) for the general population of the province:

Armenians
  Apostolic   65,033
  Catholic   10,016
  Protestant (4)   6,071
                                      81,120
Greeks
  Orthodox   11,632
  Catholic   8,291
                                      19,923
Syrians
  Orthodox   1,852
  Catholic   3,130
                                       4,982
  Protestants (Greek
    and Syrian)   6,000
  Latins   2,283
  Maronites   1,647
  Chaldeans   582

Muslims	759,040
Jews	11,748
Strangers	11,759
Foreigners	4,185
Total	903,269

To the 81,120 Armenians we have to add the Armenians of the
'mutasarriflik' of Dayr al-Zor who, according to Cuinet, numbered
400, most of whom were Catholic.

Armenian sources estimate the total Armenian population of the
'vilâyet' of Aleppo as twice that of the provincial 'salname'. Ormanian,
(5) followed by Lepsius, records 163,800, whereas Theodik's almanac
(6) gives 186,000. Here are the detailed statistics of Ormanian:
The 'kazas' of Aleppo, Iskenderun and Belen:

Apostolic	15,000	
Catholic	5,000	
Protestant	2,000	
		22,000

The 'sancaks' of Urfa and Dayr al-Zor:

Apostolic	24,000	
Catholic	1,000	
Protestant	800	
		25,800

The 'kazas' of Maraş, Elbistan and Pazarcik

Apostolic	30,000	
Catholic	4,000	
Protestant	3,500	
		37,500

The 'kazas' of Süleymanli and Andirin and the 'nahiye' of Firnis

Apostolic	27,000	
Catholic	500	
Protestant	500	
		28,000

The 'kazas' of Gaziantep and Kilis

Apostolic	30,000	
Catholic	1,000	
Protestant	4,000	
		35,000

The 'kazas' of Antioch, Jisr al-Shughûr and Sahiûn

Apostolic	12,000	
Catholic	2,000	
Protestant	1,500	
		15,500
Total		163,800

To find the most probable estimate for the Armenian population of
the 'vilâyet' of Aleppo, I have taken as I did for the other provinces, the mean of the two extreme figures; which is 133,560.

TRADES AND PROFESSIONS OF ARMENIANS

In the nineteenth century Aleppo was the centre of trading for
Northern Mesopotamia and Northern Syria, especially about 1880 when

she had a commercial revival in both imports and exports.   In 1860
the British Consul T.H. Skene reporting about the traders and
craftsmen of the province of Aleppo wrote the following:
> All the proprietors in the country are Mussulmans.   Almost all
> the traders in the towns are Christians.   Almost all the cultiva-
> tors are Mussulmans, and the pastoral tribes of Arabs, Kurds, and
> Turcomans, are nominally Mussulmans.   Almost all the manufactur-
> ing population is Christian. (7)

Armenians in the towns were practising different trades and professions, and in the villages they were engaged in agriculture.   Their
popular handicrafts were sewing and shoe-making, the fur and silk
trade, painting and tanning, the goldsmith's art and watch making.
Surmeyan, speaking of the traders of Aleppo, attests:
> Since the eighteenth century the main business of the Armenians
> who immigrated from Asia Minor to Aleppo has been sewing, and
> skilled sewers not only reached respected positions as the
> private tailors of the 'valis' succeeding one the other, and
> other government officials, but they also provided the clothing
> of the army.   Together with sewing we can remember also the
> preparation of furs....   Aleppo from old times was renowned for
> every sort of textile, especially silk, and we know that in the
> sixteenth and seventeenth centuries Aleppo had been a large
> market for silk and that the textile trade was in the hands of
> the Armenians, with wide connections extending from China to
> Holland. (8)

What is said concerning the city of Aleppo, goes also for the other
parts of the province.   For instance Farley, in his study of the resources of Turkey, testifies the following about the important role
of the Armenians in the industry and trade of Maraş:
> They [the Armenians] are the most industrious portion of the
> inhabitants of Marash, a large proportion being engaged in
> carrying on a commerce with Aleppo and Aintab;   each merchant
> keeps his own shop, where he sells his merchandise, either whole-
> sale or retail, but five or six only aspire to the title of
> wholesale merchants. (9)

From the witness quoted above one can conclude how useful the
Armenians of the 'vilâyet' of Aleppo were also in the trades and
professions of the Ottoman Empire.

CENTRES OF ARMENIAN PARTICIPATION

Under the Ottoman dominion the province of Aleppo included parts of
the Armenian kingdom of Cilicia (Little Armenia), namely the 'kazas'
of Gaziantep and Belen in the 'sancak' of Aleppo;   the whole
'sancak' of Maraş, and the 'kaza' of Urfa and Halfeti (Rumkale) in
the 'sancak' of Urfa.   These territories had been populated by
Armenians since the eleventh century, and in the nineteenth century
they were real Armenian centres.   Probably this fact has influenced
the amount of Armenian participation in local public life, because
there were many Armenian officials engaged in government duties.
    It is noticeable that a comparatively large proportion of the
Armenians of the 'kaza' of Süleymanli (Zeytun) were in public
office.   The reason for this could have been the freedom-loving

spirit of the Armenians of Zeytun with which in 1860, 1862 and
1895-6 they faced the oppressing activity of the Ottoman Government,
or perhaps it was the intervention of the European Powers that
assured more privileges for them.

During the period 1860-1908 there were not many Armenian inhabitants in the southern and eastern regions of Aleppo. Because of
this we do not find many Armenian public officials in the 'kazas' of
Jabal Sam'ân, Hârem, Idleb, Jisr al-Shughûr, Ma'arrat ul-Nu'mân,
Bâb-Jabbûl, Manbij, and Rakkah. The same was true in the
'mutasarriflik' of Dayr al-Zor since there were only 400 Armenians
living there and very few of them worked in the government.

MAIN FIELDS OF ARMENIAN PARTICIPATION

Usually the participation of Armenians in Ottoman public life was
especially marked in the provincial centres, but in the 'vilâyet'
of Aleppo the situation was different. At the headquarters of the
province and in the centre of the 'sancak' of Urfa the Armenian
officials were not more numerous than in the other outlying 'kazas'.
Only in the central 'sancak' of Maraş the Armenians were predominant
compared with the related 'kazas', but even in this case, the 'kaza'
of Süleymanli (Zeytun) shows a pre-eminent position.

In the centre of the province, at Aleppo, one could usually find
in the administrative council an Armenian elected member beside
other Christian and Muslim officials. There were only a few ex
officio members. In 1882-3 an Armenian Catholic was an ex officio
member of the local council. In the other parts of the 'vilâyet',
normally one or two but sometimes three Armenian members were
elected to the administrative councils. In Gaziantep and Maraş,
apart from the elected members there were sometimes also some ex
officio members. As for the municipal councils there were one or
two Armenian members, but again in Gaziantep, Belen, Birecik and
Maraş there were often three. As usual, they were always ordinary
officials, and only occasionally was an Armenian appointed as mayor.

In financial spheres most of the Armenians were in the taxation
department, in the tax collecting board, 'régie', and public debt
administration. With regard to taxation there was one Armenian
official in the department of each 'kaza' and he was usually the
cashier. Scarcely ever was an Armenian the head of a department,
although one was in 1873-4 in the 'kaza' of Belen; or assistant to
the head, as in 1889-90 in the 'kaza' of Iskenderun. In 'régie' the
Armenian officials were comparatively more numerous, there being
from one to three. In these departments the clerk and the storekeeper were very often Armenians, and sometimes so was the manager,
as in 1889-90 and 1898-9 in Iskenderun; in 1902-3 in Birecik, and
in 1908 in Andirin. Normally one or two Armenians could be found in
the branches of Agricultural Bank, employed as cashier or account's
clerk. The 'kaza' of Gaziantep had an Armenian manager in 1896-7,
1898-9 and 1908. In public debt administration also the Armenians
numbered one or two and usually held the offices of clerk, cashier
and accountant. In 1908 at the 'kaza' of Kilis, and in 1896-7 at
Antioch the chief officials of the public debt administration were
Armenian. Apart from these departments Armenians were from time to

time employed as tax-collectors and as officials of the branches of the Ottoman Bank, but these were only in Aleppo and Urfa. In the centres of the three 'sancaks' they were also included in the chambers of commerce.

In judicature the Armenians took part in different offices, but the main departments where they worked regularly were the courts of first instance and of commerce. In the court of first instance of every 'kaza' there was normally an Armenian as well as the Turkish member. In the commercial courts there were up to three Armenians who acted as members or clerks. At Aleppo there were usually two Armenian judges in the court of appeal, one in the civil and one in the criminal department. Other judicial duties which the Armenians carried out were the office of 'juge d'instruction', lawyer, judicial inspector, notary and clerk. In Aleppo, in 1878-9, the judicial inspector, and, in 1902-3, the lawyers were Armenian. At Gaziantep in 1896-7, 1898-9 and in 1902-3, the notaries were also Armenian.

As for the public health at Aleppo, the Armenians rendered notable service in the infirmary and military hospital, especially during the years 1896-7, 1902-3 and 1908. They held positions of doctors and chemists. In 1908 the surgeon of the infirmary was a certain Sarkis Efendi and the chemist Bedros Efendi Mazlumian. In the 'kazas' of Gaziantep and Antioch, and at the centre of the 'sancak' of Maraş, the municipal doctors were often Armenian, as were sometimes the chemists. At Maraş Doctor Kevork Efendi was employed by the municipality from about 1873 until 1889-90. In the other 'kazas' also there were Armenian doctors, chemists and vaccinators who worked in the public health departments but they were not many and their service does not appear to have been long-lasting.

OTHER FIELDS OF ARMENIAN PARTICIPATION

Other fields of Armenian participation in the province of Syria were in technical affairs, the secretariat, education and agriculture. At Aleppo in the postal and telegraphic service there were almost always from two to five Armenians who served as mechanics or tele-graph superintendents. For instance, in 1908 Krikor and Nerses Efendis were working at the section of foreign languages and were assisted by Tchakir and Asadurian Efendis. Armenians were also employed in the provincial printing house as mechanics, compositors and editors. In 1284H/1867-8 Ahmed Cevdet Paşa, the 'vali' of Aleppo and an historian, established the weekly newspaper 'Ghadîr al-Furat' ('The Rivulet of Euphrates') in which the news, orders and declarations of the government were published in Arabic and Turkish. In 1286H/1869-70 it was called just 'al-Furât' ('The Euphrates') and a new section in Armenian was added. This newspaper continued until 1918 but the Armenian part, for reasons unknown to me, lasted only one and a half years. (10)

At Gaziantep in 1882-3 and 1902-3 the municipal engineers were Armenian, and in 1898-9 two members were included on the public works' board. In 1889-90 at the 'kazas' of Belen and Iskenderun the postmen were Armenian; and in Maraş and Urfa one or two members

sometimes sat on the board of public works. In connection with the
secretariat it must be said that the Armenian officials in the
different departments of public affairs were often given the duty of
clerk or accountant. Likewise in Aleppo, Iskenderun and Belen some
Armenians were engaged in the purely secretarial departments, e.g.
chief secretariat, land registry and customs administration. In
1873-4 the assistant translator of the province was an Armenian.
    With regard to agriculture at Aleppo, in 1896-7 and 1908 the
model-farm managers were Armenian. In the 'kazas' of Gaziantep,
Belen, Iskenderun, and at the centres of the 'sancaks' of Maraş and
Urfa, one or two Armenian members sometimes sat on the forestry
board and on the boards of trade and agriculture. In the sphere of
education Armenians were included on the education council, in the
secondary school and in school of handicrafts at the centres of the
'sancaks'. At Aleppo, as in the centres of some other provinces the
Armenian language was taught in the government's secondary school
from about 1898-9 until 1908. In 1908 the teacher of carpet weaving
in the handicrafts school of Aleppo was Akob Agha, and in the
preparatory school for girls Aznivuhi was the lady-teacher of
'hüner' (art). Again in the same year at Urfa a certain Akob Agha
taught the blacksmith's art and shoe-making, while Karapet Imirzian
was on the school board.

ARMENIAN PARTICIPATION IN ZEYTUN

In the second half of the nineteenth century the Armenians of Zeytun
(now Süleymanli) enjoyed a comparatively advantageous position in
the public life of the district. This is why I describe here the
part of Armenians in the governmental affairs of Zeytun. In the
administrative council of the 'kaza' the Armenians were represented
by two or three elected members. In addition to these there were
sometimes two Armenian ex officio members, one Apostolic and one
Catholic. After 1896 the governors ('kaymakam') were Christian,
most of them being Greek. The municipal administration was almost
entirely in the hands of the Armenian officials. There were between
three and six members and from 1896 the mayor was also Armenian. In
the years 1898-9 and 1908 there were no Turks at all, and in 1902-3
only the clerk was Turkish. Armenians were influential in the
administration of the 'nahiye' of Firnis also, having usually two
members on the council. After 1896 the administrator of this
commune was sometimes Armenian as well. There was always an
Armenian member beside the Turkish on the trial council or on the
court of first instance. From time to time the notary was also
Armenian, and in 1896-7 an Armenian held the position of assistant
'juge d'instruction'.
    Armenians participated extensively in matters of finance. In the
administration of public finance the cashier was normally Armenian,
as was sometimes the assistant to the head. In 'régie' the administrator was often Armenian, being the sole official of the chamber.
At the branch of the Agricultural Bank, there were two or three
Armenian members and after 1896 the chief manager was often
Armenian, as in 1896-7, 1902-3 and 1908.
    The Armenians of Zeytun also participated in other fields of

public life, such as in agriculture and technical works, but since such affairs in an outlying 'kaza' were not extensive their part was not great.

COMPARATIVE NOTE: GREEK PARTICIPATION

Greek participation in the public life of this province was neither large nor constant but we do find some Greek officials in different governmental departments. Their contribution to public affairs was notable mainly in the 'sancak' of Aleppo, and particularly in the town of Aleppo itself. Here at the provincial headquarters one or two Greeks occasionally worked in the administrative council, in the courts of appeal and trade, in the administration of finance and the branches of the Agricultural Bank, at the public works department and the postal and telegraphic service, in the military hospital and in the state secondary school. Outside Aleppo, in the 'kazas' of Iskenderun, Idleb, and Antioch, Greeks were sometimes included on the administrative councils as elected members, in the municipalities as doctors, in the courts of first instance as judges, in the Agricultural Bank's branches as cashiers or clerks, and in the postal and telegraphic service as telegraph superintendents in the section for foreign languages.

In the 'sancak' of Urfa, Greek participation in public life would be found mainly at the centre of the county and in the 'kaza' of Birecik, as members of commercial court and as cashiers or clerks in financial administration. There was only one of them in each department. In the 'sancak' of Maraş, at the centre of the county and in Elbistan occasionally Greek officials were employed as municipal doctors or chemists, and after 1896 the governor of the 'kaza' of Süleymanli was usually Greek.

A GENERAL VIEW OF ARMENIAN PARTICIPATION IN THE PROVINCE OF ALEPPO

In the province of Aleppo, the Armenian participation in Ottoman public life was especially notable and constant in the city of Aleppo itself and in that part of the 'vilâyet' called the 'sancak' of Maraş which in the middle ages once belonged to the Armenian kingdom of Cilicia. From a chronological point of view the Armenians were given a larger part and higher positions in the different governmental units of the province after 1896. The main fields of public life in which the Armenians took part were the political administration, finance, judicial courts and the public health service. In these departments of the 'vilâyet' there were usually to be found one or two, but sometimes three or four, Armenian officials.

SOME NOTABLE ARMENIANS IN THE PUBLIC LIFE OF THE PROVINCE OF ALEPPO

ABRAHAMIAN, Yaruthiwn (?-1895). An Armenian Protestant chemist who worked in the municipality of Urfa.
ARIKIAN, Yaruthiwn (1815-90). Born in Maraş, he was a merchant and

on very friendly terms with the Turks. For thirty-eight years he
acted as a member of the administrative council. He was honoured by
the Sublime Porte with the 'Mecidiye' and 'Osmaniye' orders of the
third class.

ATTARIAN, Abraham (?-1915). A Protestant Armenian of renown in
Urfa. 'For many years' he was the chemist of the German Hospital
and at the same time he served on the local municipal council.

AYVAZIAN, Krikor (?-1900). Born in Urfa, he learned Armenian and
Turkish, and became a shopkeeper. One of his customers, a 'binbaşi'
(battalion commander) recognized his cleverness and invited him to
go with him to Dayr al-Zor and become a purveyor of food for the
army. Ayvazian thus went to serve the Ottoman army (c. 1885) in
which he was accorded the rank of 'kol agasi' (adjutant major). In
1895-6, at the time of the massacres, he returned home with the same
'binbaşi' and saved his parents and about 1,000 other people. After
the atrocities he returned with his brother to Dayr al-Zor and
continued his work.

BARSUMIAN, Baghdasar. Born in Gaziantep, he studied medicine in the
American University of Beirut. In 1897, after graduating, he
settled in Kilis where he was appointed municipal doctor. He left
Kilis in 1903.

BASMADJIAN, Armenak. Born and brought up in Kilis, from 1906 to
1910 he was a finance administration agent there.

BASMADJIAN, Ghazar (Lazar). He was a member of the administrative
council at the 'kaza' of Kilis from 1885 to 1914.

BAYRAMIAN, Kevork. From 1885 to 1905 he was a member of the
administrative council in Kilis.

DER-BEDROSIAN (Ter-Petrosian), Aghadjan. An educated and clever
merchant of Urfa who was in the import and export business with his
brother Nishan. He was elected member to the criminal and commercial courts. About the beginning of the twentieth century he acted
as assistant mayor and also supplied provisions for the army.

DJANSIZIAN, Martiros. Originally from Maraş, he came to Kilis in
1905 and was appointed manager of the public debt administration.
He carried out this office until 1912.

GUIRAGOSIAN (Kirakosian), Martiros (?-1909). Until 1909 he was a
member of the administrative council of Antioch.

GÜLÜZIAN, Kevork (c. 1840-95). Was born and educated in Maraş where
he practised medicine for some years as medical officer of health to
the municipality. During the cholera epidemic of 1890 he saved many
lives by using the Hamlyn mixture.

HEKIMIAN, Sarkis. Son of Kevork, he was a municipal and military
doctor in Gaziantep. Being a well-known figure he was appointed to
this office by a special Imperial order. He lived in the nineteenth
century but no dates for his life are recorded.

IMIRZIAN, Karapet (?-1915). Born and educated in Urfa, he was a
merchant and possessed villages which were cultivated by Armenian as
well as Kurdish and Arab peasants. From 1895 he was a member of the
local administrative council and in 1903 was appointed to the court
of justice. At the same time he directed the financial administration of the Turkish Hospital and the government secondary school at
Urfa.

ISHKHANIAN, Iskender. Born in Gaziantep in 1893, he settled in
Aleppo where he was appointed municipal doctor. He carried out this

office 'until his death' (?). His son Nuri was also a military
doctor from 1919 to 1923.

KADEHDJIAN, Sarkis (c. 1830-1907). A self-trained architect in
Gaziantep who built several caravanserais and churches, like, for
example, the large and beautiful church of S. Astvadzadzin (Mother
of God). 'For many years' he was a governmental chief architect.

KARGODORIAN, Sarkis (1854-?). Born in Maraş he learned masonry from
his father and developing his craft became an architect. He built
the barracks at Maraş and Süleymanli as well as some Armenian
churches. After the great fire of 1884 in Maraş he restored the
Eski and built the Yeni covered markets, the Municipal market, and
the 'hans' (inn, large commercial building) of Tuz and Hişir. He
also repaired three bridges on the river Aksu and two on the Ceyhan.
During the First World War he fled to Lebanon and settled in Beirut.

KEYIKIAN, Krikor (1855-1916). He was born and educated in Maraş
where he became a tradesman. For about twenty-five years he was a
member of the local administrative council. He also acted as an
agent for the American and German Missionaries in their dealings
with the government.

KHIRLAKIAN, Yakob (1856-1920). An Armenian Catholic merchant who
was army contractor in Maraş. He received honours both from the
Sublime Porte and Pope Leo XIII.

KIREMITDJIAN, Boghos (fl.c. 1900). He was a veterinary surgeon in
the army at Aleppo and was a censor at the same time.

MAHIKIAN, Thoros (1862-1916). Born in Maraş and educated in local
Armenian schools, he learned Turkish and worked in government
departments as a clerk and as an official of the judicial court of
first instance. From 1880 onwards in addition to these functions he
taught Turkish in Armenian schools.

MAKSUDIAN Efendi. From about 1900 to 1908 he was a provincial
forest inspector of the 'vilâyet' of Aleppo.

MANUSHAKIAN, Nazareth (1874-1933). Born in Gaziantep, he studied in
the Armenian Vardanean School. After finishing his studies he was
engaged in trade, mainly importing paints. He was a member of the
commercial court. In 1921 he settled in Aleppo.

MELITOSIAN, Levon. From about 1895 until 1915 he was a municipal
doctor in Süleymanli.

MOMDJIAN, Sarkis. About 1895 (until 1915?) he was a manager of the
'régie' in Süleymanli.

MURADIAN, Kevork (1831-94). Born in Maraş, he worked as a weaver
while studying Turkish literature and the legal code. For about
thirty years he was a member of the civil court, and a government
lawyer as well. He owned land and was influential in government
circles, but (according to our source) because he publicly accused
the officials of bribery and staunchly defended the rights of his
compatriots, he was deposed from his judicial post in 1892.

NALTCHADJIAN, Karapet (1862-1916). He was born in Maraş and
educated in the local schools of the Armenians and of the Franciscan
Fathers. He also studied the Turkish legal code on his own and was
afterwards appointed chief clerk in the criminal court. For two
years he was the 'juge d'instruction' of the 'kaza' of Andirin in
Maraş, and later worked as a lawyer in Maraş for twelve years.

NORASHKHARHIAN, Babik (?-1886). A notable man of the Armenian community of Süleymanli. From 1879 he was the mayor of the district.

NORASHKHARHIAN, Kevork. The son of Shil-Panos, from 1869 to 1883 he was the chief of the police in Süleymanli.

SHATAREVIAN, Thoros (1854-1924). An Armenian Catholic born and educated in the Armenian schools at Maraş, he took private lessons in Turkish from the Çitilci Hocas. In 1870 he was employed as chief clerk in the town courts of justice and commerce. In 1881 he went to Aleppo and, having passed the legal examinations, became a lawyer. Thereafter he practised his profession in Aleppo and was appointed president of its trial board. He was honoured by the Sublime Porte with the 'Mecidiye' order of the second class.

TASHDJIAN, Yakob (?-1915). The son of the architect Khatcher in Urfa, he was influential in the Armenian community as well as in the government. 'For many years' he participated in the court of justice as a member. He also presided over a conciliation committee whose function was to settle differences between the Kurdish and Arab tribes around Urfa.

TOPALIAN, Yovhannes. Originally from Maraş where he was a member of the administrative council. In 1895 he moved to Gaziantep and worked there first as the manager of the 'régie' and then as a lawyer.

Chapter 10

THE ARMENIANS OF SYRIA II. DAMASCUS, BEIRUT AND MOUNT LEBANON

HISTORICAL SURVEY

This chapter describes the Armenian participation in Ottoman public life of littoral Syria and the region of Damascus (Dimeshq), as well as of the province of Beirut (Bayrût) and the 'mutasarriflik' of Jabal Lubnân (Ott.Turk. Cebel-i Lübnân).

Beirut, a Phoenician town, mentioned in history as early as the Tell ul-Amârinah tablets, has been and is a centre of learning and commerce. It passed from the Greeks and Romans to the Arabs and then to the Crusaders. During the Turkish period it was possessed by the 'âmirs' of the house of Ma'n of whom was the famous Druse (Durzî) prince Fakhr al-Dîn (1595-1634). It was brought under the direct Turkish rule in 1763. Until 1888 it formed a part of the province of Syria, then it was made a separate 'vilâyet' including the 'sancaks' of Beirut, Tripoli, Lâdhikiyye,'Akka and Nablos.

Jabal Lubnân (Mount Lebanon) sometimes referred to as Lebanon, was at the beginning of our period, 1840-60, a theatre of fighting between the Maronites (Mârunî) and Druses. (1) The disturbance ended in 1860 in the massacre of Maronites whereupon the French forces intervened to re-establish peace. Fuad Paşa (1814-68) was sent from the Porte as a plenipotent representative. Among the attendants of the Paşa were the following Armenians: Isahak Abro Efendi and Stephan Arzumanian as secretaries, Rizqâllah Hassûn al-Halabî as translator, Dr Serovbê Vitchênian, Dr Nahapet Russinian, and Dr Gabriel Sevian.

In order to prevent any further turmoil, an international commission was assigned to achieve a 'Règlement organique' to offer the Mount Lebanon a semi-independence under the control of the Powers. As a result of the European intervention Jabal Lubnân was made a separate 'mutasarriflik' attached directly to the Porte. The 'mutasarrif' would be a Christian and act for three years on the approval of the Powers. Thus the first governor came to be Davud Paşa, an Armenian from Istanbul, whose office was prolonged for another five years until 1868. From this new regulation emerged the modern Lebanon which traditionally has a Christian president as the head of the Republic.

As to the Armenians, they were related with Lebanon about 84-70

BC, when the armies of the King Tigran the Great conquered the larger parts of Syria, Phoenicia and Palestine. The Armenians came in close contact with Lebanon especially after the creation of the Armenian kingdom of Cilicia. But until the eighteenth century the Armenian inhabitants there were few. In 1721, under the leadership of Abraham Muradian (1663-1738), an Armenian Catholic brotherhood of St Anton was established on Mount Lebanon, at Kureym (near the village of Ghosta), which in 1750 got another monastery in Beit Khashbo, near Ghazir. At the same time the patriarchate of the Armenian Catholics of Syria, created in 1772, was founded in Bzommar. (2) Apart from being a religious centre this monastery became a shelter for the Armenians who left Turkey for political reasons. This encouraged their settlement in Lebanon. The Armenians increased in number during the troubles in Anatolia in 1894-6, but above all during the First World War when many refugees came and settled in and around Beirut. Lebanon has now the most vigorous and active community of the Armenian Diaspora.

ADMINISTRATIVE STRUCTURE

The provinces of Damascus and Beirut, and the independent 'mutasarriflik' of Jabal Lubnân are considered here together, as the rest of Syria, because in the second half of the nineteenth century not very many Armenians lived in these regions. The province of Damascus had four 'sancaks', Damascus, Hamah, Hauran, al-Salt, and twenty-two 'kazas' as the following.
The 'kazas' of the 'sancak' of Damascus:
    Damascus
    Duma
    Nabak
    Ba'labakka (Baalbek)
    Rashayya
    Hasbayya
    al-Biqa' ul-Azîzî
    Wâdî' al-Adjam
The 'kazas' of the 'sancak' of Hamah:
    Hamah
    Hims
    al-Salamayya
    Hamidiyya
The 'kazas' of the 'sancak' of Hauran:
    Hauran
    Knaytra
    Basra'l Harîr
    Dar'a
    Jabal al-Drûz
    Adjlûn
The 'kazas' of the 'sancak' of al-Salt (now in Jordan):
    al-Salt
    al-Karak
    al-Tufayla
    Ma'ân
The province of Beirut had five 'sancaks', Lâdhikiyya, Beirut,

Tripoli, 'Akka, Nablos, and twenty-one 'kazas' as the following:
The 'kazas' of the 'sancak' of al-Lâdhikiyya:
   al-Lâdhikiyya
   Jabla
   Markab
   Sahiûn
The 'kazas' of Beirut:
   Beirut
   Sur
   Sayda
   Merdj 'Ayûn
The 'kazas' of the 'sancak' of Tripoli:
   Tripoli
   'Akkar
   Safita
   Husn al-Akrâd (Qal'at ul-Husn)
The 'kazas' of the 'sancak' of 'Akka:
   'Akka
   Hayfa
   Tabariyya
   al-Nasira
   Safad
The 'kazas' of the 'sancak' of Nablos:
   Nablos
   Jabîn Saltî
   Bani Sa'ab
   Jamâ'în
The 'mutasarriflik' of Mount Lebanon included these 'kazas':
   al-Shuf
   al-Metn
   al-Batrun
   Jezzin
   Zahlah
   Kisruan
   al-Kura
   Deir al-Qamar ('müdüriyet')

POPULATION

In the nineteenth century the Armenian population of the littoral
Syria, the district of Damascus and of Lebanon was not numerous.
They increased after the First World War when many of them were
transported into the Syrian deserts. Some of them fled or moved
from Syria to Lebanon where there are now about 200,000 Armenians.
   The year-book of the province of Syria (or Damascus) for 1900-1
records the following concerning the Armenian population:
   Damascus

Apostolic	257	
Catholic	179	
		436
Wâdî' al-Adjam		
Apostolic		52
Rashayya		
Catholic		30

Hamah
    Apostolic   5

                    Total   523

Ormanian, (3) followed by Lepsius, gives the number of the Armenians of the 'vilâyet' of Syria as 2,000 which is much higher than the figures of the 'salname' of 1900-1. Cuinet also records the Armenian population as 2,025, a number which is in close agreement with Ormanian's figures. (4)

As to Lebanon, the sources account the Armenian population of the province of Beirut as about 1,200-1,300. Ormanian estimates the number of the Armenians as 1,300 (1,000 Apostolic and 300 Catholic), while the provincial 'salname' of 1908 gives 1,218. (5) These are the detailed statistics of the year-book:

Beirut
    Apostolic   108
    Catholic   461
                              569
Tripoli
    Catholic   14
Lâdhikiyya
    Catholic   243
Sahiûn   392

                    Total   1,218

In Jabal Lubnân it would appear that there were very few Armenians. The year-book of this 'mutasarriflik' records the number of the Armenians as about 5 together with the Syrians (Christian) in the 'kaza' of Kisruan. Possibly there were also Armenians accounted among Protestants, who are estimated to be 167. It is interesting and a little astonishing that Ormanian, (6) followed by Lepsius, presents the approximate number of the Armenians of Jabal Lubnân and of Jerusalem as 3,200 (3,000 Apostolic, 200 Catholic). If about 2,000 of those lived in Jerusalem, as it is said in Theodik's almanac, (7) then one would conclude that there were 1,000 or 1,200 Armenians in Jabal Lubnân, but unfortunately we do not have any other source to ascertain this information. To sum up, again we would take the mean of the two antipodal numbers. The Armenians of littoral Syria, Damascus, Beirut and Jabal Lubnân, according to the Turkish 'salnames' were about 1,800, and according to Ormanian as 4,500. The mean of these figures, 3,150, possibly gives the best estimate of the Armenian population.

TRADES AND PROFESSIONS OF ARMENIANS

In the second half of the nineteenth century, the Armenians of Syria were occupied in agriculture, crafts and trade. The main produce of this province were: wheat, barley, maize, rice, cotton, sugar-cane, tobacco, vegetables and fruits, timber, limestone, slate, coal, iron and copper. The leather work of Damascus was (and still is) popular, while wood and metal inlaid work was exported to other countries.

The Armenians of the 'vilâyet' of Syria were more industrious and

prosperous before 1860, when the Christians were tortured and
massacred in Damascus and Jabal Lubnân. At that time, apparently,
some Armenians were troubled but others escaped. Ephrikian,
speaking especially of the Armenians of Damascus, attests the
following:

> In Damascus before the massacres of 1860, there were about 30
> naturalized Armenian families and quite a few alien merchants.
> But from those at this time [i.e. 1897/8], have remained only
> five families, and none is engaged in trade. Now the Armenians
> are about 40 houses, approximately 300 persons, immigrated from
> different towns, who hardly earn their daily living. (8)

The Armenians of Lebanon were engaged in different professions and
trades. This is the conclusion of Varjapetian who has studied the
history of the Armenians there:

> Before 1895, the Armenian community of Lebanon was composed of
> 30-40 houses, that means, approximately there were about 200
> Apostolic Armenians in the whole of the province. There were
> about the same number of Catholic Armenians. The Armenians were
> generally state officials of high ranks and renowned merchants,
> who enjoyed an exceptional position here, being respected both by
> the Turkish government and by the natives. (9)

Among the numerous Armenian merchants of Beirut we can mention the
following as very active and well-known tradesmen who flourished
about 1890: Bedros (Petros) Aghadjanian, Sarkis Eghiayan, Gabriel
Gabrielian, Tigran Kalemkarian, Tigran Kasardjian, Meguerditch
Hazarapetian, Yovhannes Gülbenkian, Yakob Mukhtarian, Nazareth
Baghdasarian (Baltasarian), Barsum Petrosian, Stephan Topuzkhanian,
and Khirlakian family.

CENTRES OF ARMENIAN PARTICIPATION

In the province of Syria the centres of Armenian participation were:
Damascus, Ba'labakka and Rashayya in the 'sancak' of Damascus;
Hamah and Hims in the 'sancak' of Hamah, and the 'kaza' of Adjlûn in
the 'sancak' of Hauran. There were no Armenian officials in the
'sancak' of Salt.

In the 'vilâyet' of Beirut, the Armenians worked in the departments of the central government, in the 'kaza' of Tripoli at the
'sancak' of Tripoli, in 'Akka and Safad of the 'sancak' of 'Akka,
and at the centres of the 'sancak' of Lâdhikiyya and Nablos. As to
the 'mutasarriflik' of Jabal Lubnân, Armenian officials in public
life would be found, apart from in the centre, only at the 'kazas'
of Shuf and Zahlah.

ARMENIAN PARTICIPATION IN THE PUBLIC LIFE OF THE PROVINCE OF
DAMASCUS

In the province of Damascus the Armenians took part mainly in the
departments of finance, engineering and the public health service.
At the headquarters of the 'vilâyet', in 1888-9 the Agricultural
Bank agent was an Armenian, as was the accountant of the Ottoman
Bank in 1900-1. In the technical field, in 1888-9 there were an

Armenian engineer and a foreman in the department of public works;
in 1895-6 the assistant engineer was a certain Tigran Efendi;   in
1900-1 Shahin Efendi was the assistant engineer, while Melkon
Sukiasian, who between 1892 and 1903 was the agricultural inspector,
became an engineer of mining from 1904 to 1908.   In 1883-4 the
forestry agent was an Armenian, Boghos Efendi.

In the spheres of public health, at the military hospital, in
1878-9 the surgeon was Yovhannes Efendi;   in 1888-9 the chemist and
adjutant-major doctor were Armenian;   in 1895-6 Artin Efendi was a
major doctor and Martiros Efendi was a hospital warder, but in
1900-1 the chemist of the municipality was Ohannes Efendi.   As to
education, in 1900-1 the vice-director of the government secondary
school was Hambartzum Efendi Nizamian who at the same time taught
arithmetic, cosmology, chemistry and engineering.   At the 'kaza' of
Ba'labakka the controller of revenue and expenditure was Armenian in
1888-9.   In 1900-1 the department of 'régie' there was an
Armenian official, and at the branch of the Agricultural Bank in
1895-6 and 1900-1 the accountant was Armenian.   In Duma, in 1883-4
the controller of revenue and expenditure was Iskender Kevorkian
Efendi, who in the capacity of his office was also ex officio member
to the administrative council.

At Nabak in 1888-9 the title-deeds' clerk was Armenian, and from
about 1878 to 1895-6 there was an Armenian member in the administrative council of the 'kaza' of Rashayya.   In the centre of the
'sancak' of Hamah an Armenian was elected to the administrative
council in 1869-70, and in 1900-1 the municipal chemist was Petros
Efendi.   At the 'kaza' of Hims about 1869-84 there was an Armenian
member in the municipal council and in 1900-1 a member was in the
administrative council.   In Adjlûn in the 'sancak' of Hauran, in
1900-1 the municipal doctor was Mihran Efendi Petrosian (Bedrosian).

ARMENIAN PARTICIPATION IN THE PUBLIC LIFE OF THE PROVINCE OF BEIRUT

The participation of Armenians in the public life of Beirut was most
evident at the centre of the province.   They worked in the departments of technical affairs, public finance, the public health service, the judicature, education and agriculture.   In the engineering
department the engineers in 1900-1 and 1908 were Armenian, Yovhannes
and Vitchên Efendis, and from 1892 to 1901 the foremen were also
Armenian.   In 1908 there was an agent in the postal and telegraphic
service, while in 1893-4 the postmaster was Hambartzum Efendi.   At
the state press in 1893-4 the chief compositor was Armenian.

In 1908 in the public debt administration the first accountant's
clerk was Armenian and in the customs-house the chief clerk was
Armenian.   In 1900-1 the agent for the forest and mine inspectorship
was Oskan Efendi and from 1905 to 1908 Yakob Efendi Aslanian was the
agricultural inspector.   In judicature, from 1900 to 1902 a certain
Krikor Efendi was included on the commercial court and during 1905-6
Arthur Efendi Maghachian was the judicial inspector.   In the sphere
of education the accounts keeper of the education council was
Armenian in 1893-4, as were the first and second assistants of the
director in the state secondary school.   From about 1900 to 1908
Ervand (Yervant) Karakashian lectured in the same school in French,

general history, law, book-keeping and astronomy, and in 1901-2
Ervand Damghadjian taught geography, book-keeping and chemistry.
In connection with the health service the Armenians contributed
much particularly after 1890. In the military hospital from about
1888 to 1894 an Armenian, Mihran Efendi, was surgeon, and from 1900
to 1908 Tigran Efendi was the chemist. In 1893-4 there were three
Armenian doctors in the army medical corps. In 1900-1, Arshak
Efendi was health inspector for animals, and in the same year
Aristakes Efendi was clerk of French in the quarantine department.
Among the practising doctors of Beirut, the provincial year-book of
1908 records the name of Yuhanna Wortabed (Yovhannes Vardapet), and
among the graduated chemists Eduar(d) Tokatli (Tokatlian). At
'Akka, an Armenian was quarantine agent from about 1893/4 to 1908.
In the 'kazas' of Tabariyya and Nasira in 1900-2 the postmasters
were Armenian, being Parsegh Efendi and Ervand Efendi, respectively.
Likewise at Safad in 1893-4 the postmaster was an Armenian, while in
the same district Nishan Efendi was the municipal doctor in 1901.
In Tripoli in 1893-4 Markar Efendi was the quarantine doctor and
Yovhannes Efendi was the engineer of public works from 1900 to 1902.
In 1893-4 at the postal and telegraphic service of the quay the
chief agent was an Armenian, Bedros Efendi. At the centre of the
'sancak' of Nablos in 1893-4 there was an Armenian in the administrative council; from 1900 to 1901 the municipal doctors were
Armenian, viz. Artin and Nishan Efendis and from about 1893-4 to
1900-1 an agent of the Agricultural Bank branch was Miridjan Efendi
(Armenian?).
In Lâdhikiyya (now in Syria) some Armenians worked in the postal
and telegraphic service during the period of 1878-9 to 1901-2, and
from 1869-70 to 1878-9 an Armenian was included on the judicial
council. At the 'kaza' of Jabla, in 1901-2 Mattheos Efendi was the
municipal doctor.

ARMENIAN PARTICIPATION IN THE PUBLIC LIFE OF JABAL LUBNÂN

The part of Armenians in the public life of Jabal Lubnân was very
limited, possibly because there were very few of them living in this
'mutasarriflik'. In the chief secretariat of the central government, Krikor Efendi Küpelian was the head of clerks from 1888 to
1892. At the same time there was an Armenian copyist in that
office. Again, during 1888-92 the postmaster was Armenian. At
Zahlah in 1878-9 the chief official of the postal and telegraphic
service was Yovhannes Efendi. In 1888-9 in the municipal council of
the 'nahiya' of Akiba there was an Armenian member.

A GENERAL VIEW OF ARMENIAN PARTICIPATION

Armenian participation in the public affairs of the provinces of
Damascus and Beirut was not very large or constant and, especially
in Jabal Lubnân, Armenians had very little part in the public
administrative apparatus. The reason, I think, was that the
Armenians of these districts were few in number, viz. 3,150. Comparing the number of Armenian participants in Ottoman public life

with the total number of Armenian inhabitants one can rightly conclude that they were well treated. But why was this? Possibly
because the Armenians were an industrious element, or it could also
be that the Turks, from a political point of view, trusted them in
Syria and Lebanon. It is interesting to note that while in other
provinces Armenians were mainly included on the administrative and
municipal councils and in the courts of justice, in the 'vilâyets'
of Damascus and Beirut and in the 'mutasarriflik' of Jabal Lubnân
they acted mostly in technical departments, the health service, in
public finance and agricultural affairs. I think the reason for
this phenomenon was that for political administration and justice
the officials would be elected among the communities according to
their number, whereas the other offices were acquired through
appointment.

In the sphere of education the Armenians, due to their knowledge
of Turkish and Arabic, were employed in the government secondary
schools as vice-directors and teachers. The Armenians in
Lebanon increased after the troubles of 1915-20. Today there are
six Armenian deputies (four Armenian Apostolic, one Armenian
Catholic and one Armenian Protestant) in the Parliament and many
Armenians are employed in different fields of public life.

SOME NOTABLE ARMENIANS IN THE PUBLIC LIFE OF DAMASCUS, BEIRUT AND
MOUNT LEBANON

DAVUD Paşa, Karapet (1816-73). Born at Istanbul he was the son of
an Armenian Catholic named Artin Davud (Davudian) or Davud Oghlu.
He received his higher education in Germany at the University of
Berlin, and on his return to Istanbul he was employed in the
ministry of foreign affairs. Later he became the attaché at the
Turkish Embassy in Berlin, where he wrote a remarkable study on old
German law, 'Histoire de la législation des anciens Germains'
(Berlin, 1845), for which in August 1858 he was granted an honorary
doctorate by the faculty in law in Jena. On 7 April 1856 he was
appointed by an Imperial writ as the Ottoman general consul at
Vienna. In 1858 he became the state printing director of the
'vilâyet' of Aleppo; in 1859 the head of the department of censure
at Istanbul, and in 1860 the minister of telegraphic service. In
the middle of June 1861, at the critical situation of Lebanon, he
was assigned as the first governor general of the 'mutasarriflik' of
Jabal Lubnân (1861-3). For having shown wisdom there, his office
was prolonged for five more years (1863-8). In 1868 he became
minister of public works at Istanbul where he was successful in
managing the construction of the Rumelian railway. In 1871 he
retired, already ill, and died at Biarritz on 4 November 1873. (10)
HALEPLIAN, Daniel. Born in Arapkir and educated in the local
Armenian Catholic school, he was employed in the telegraphic service at Alacahan, Tokat and Istanbul. Later he moved to Beirut and
worked there in the postal and telegraphic service for 'twenty
years', 1905-15(?).
ISHAK, Awni (1860-1935). Born at Damascus, he became a lawyer and
served the courts of justice in Beirut and Jerusalem. He translated
the Ottoman criminal code into Arabic. For his service he was given

the order of 'Osmaniye' by the government.

KHASHO, Emil. The son of Joseph and the grandson of Antun, he came from Tiflis, but by 1820 had settled in Damascus. Emil studied constructional engineering at St Joseph University of Beirut and the University of Louvain. From 1897 to 1902 he worked in Belgium and then returned to Beirut. In 1904 he was appointed chief engineer, but he carried out his office only for three years. He constructed several buildings in Beirut of which the hospital 'Autel Dieu de France' is famous.

KHAYAT, Yovseph (Joseph). He was born in Beirut, but his ancestors were from Tiflis. In 1870 he was employed as a government engineer at Damascus and later worked in the municipality of Beirut for eighteen years.

KHENDAMIAN, Araqel (1856-1914). Born at Üsküdar, he was sent by the Ottoman Government to Russia among a group of students to learn engineering there. After obtaining his degree he was employed in Jerusalem as a government official from 1895 to 1903. In 1904 he moved into Beirut and in 1907 into Aleppo, always being a government engineer.

MANUKIAN, Manuk-Bshara (1841-1925). He learned engineering and in 1860 was employed to work on the causeway from Beirut to Damascus. On that occasion he made the acquaintance of Fuad Paşa (1814-68) who sent him to Trebizond to co-operate in the construction of the road leading to Erzurum. In 1870 he returned to Beirut and continued to work there. According to our source for 'a long time' he was chief engineer in the 'vilâyets' of Damascus and Beirut. In 1890 he directed some excavations at Sayda. For his public service he was honoured with 'five decorations' by the Ottoman Government.

MINASIAN, Petros (1881-1935). Born in Bursa, he was educated in Jerusalem in the Armenian monastery of St James and at the local French school. In 1900 he settled in Beirut where he was employed in the post as 'an official of high rank'. He carried out his office until 1914.

NAFILIAN, Kasbar (Gaspar) (1875-1938). Born at Istanbul in the family of Dr Anton, he studied architecture in Paris and finished his course in 1895. In 1902 he went to Beirut on the invitation of Muzaffar Paşa to design the plan of a government building. He remained in Lebanon and served the country in his capacity as an architect.

SUKIASIAN, Melkon (1860-1915). Born in a village of Çemişgezek (in Elâzig), he studied agronomy at Istanbul and Paris. In 1883-4 he was employed in the ministry of agriculture at Istanbul and two years later he was sent to Aleppo as the provincial administrator of agriculture. In 1892 he was transferred to Damascus where he worked first as the agricultural inspector until 1903 and then, from 1904 to 1908, as a mining engineer.

TCHADERDJIAN, Meguerditch (1870-1937). Born in Diyarbakir he learned, apart from his mother tongue, Turkish, Arabic and Persian. In 1895/6 he settled down in Beirut and for 'long years' worked there in the public debt administration.

WORTABED (VARDAPET), Yuhanna (John or Yovhannes), MD (1826-1908). Son of Yakob Wortabed, was born at Sayda in Lebanon. He learned first in a local missionary school, and then received higher education in Scotland. From 1851 to 1855 he was the parson of the

Protestant Church at Hasbayya (being ordained in May 1853). He went
back to Scotland and in 1860 published his important book,
'Researches into the Religions of Syria', drawn from original
sources. Afterwards he was sent to Aleppo as a missionary of the
United Presbyterian Church of Scotland where he acted until 1896
when he was called to a professorship in the Medical College of
Beirut (later American University of Beirut). From October 1867 to
1882 he lectured in anatomy and physiology. He was also on the
committee which organized the 'Asfuriyyah' hospital for insane.
From 1882 to 1908 he served the people as a doctor having his clinic
at Bab Idris in Beirut. He was granted decorations by the Ottoman
Government.

CONCLUSIONS

ARMENIAN PARTICIPATION IN ADMINISTRATIVE AND MUNICIPAL COUNCILS

In the public life of the Ottoman Empire the administrative councils
were the main governing bodies which acted under the presidency of
the 'valis' (provincial governors), 'mutasarrifs' (governors of
'sancak'), 'kaymakams' (governors of 'kaza') and 'müdürs' (governors
of 'nahiye'). The members of these councils came into office by
election, being representatives of Muslim and Christian communities.
Each community would have officials in the councils according to its
number. In the administrative councils the Armenians normally had
two or three representatives. At the provincial headquarters and in
the centres of the 'sancaks' there were also one or two ex officio
Armenian members who were the spiritual heads of the Apostolic and
Catholic communities. If there was a substantial Protestant community, they too were entitled to representation. This number was
increased to three if the head of the government department of
finance happened to be an Armenian. The elected Turkish and
Armenian members of the councils were usually equal in number, but
the ex officio Turkish members were always more numerous, since in
addition to the governors and muftis, the deputy judges and often
the heads of financial departments were Turks. Consequently the
Turkish members of the administrative councils were in the majority,
and the controlling power was in their hands. This is the reason
why the Armenians, in spite of their participation in political
administration, were not able to defend their lives and rights. It
might be thought that the Armenians were exaggerating their dis-
content about the Ottoman administration in Anatolia as, for
instance, in their published report on outrages, (1) and when they
demanded reforms at the Congresses of San Stefano and Berlin. But
there are eye-witness accounts by foreigners which attest to the
abnormal situation. Here is what the British Consul of Aleppo,
T.H. Skene, wrote to the Home Office:

> There are two Christian members of the 'Medjlis', but their
> presence at the sittings is a mere matter of form, as they take
> no part in deliberations and are treated with utter disregard,
> never venturing to express dissent in any decision, even though
> it be calculated to injure their brother Christians. (2)

Here is also what 'a Prussian gentleman' from Erzurum affirmed concerning the administrative councils:

> Dans chaque conseil les communautés arméniennes doivent être
> représentées: là où elles le sont, les membres chrétiens des
> conseils ne sont que des personnages muets sans aucune influence.
> (3)

It is evident that in a despotic regime like that of the Ottoman Empire the chief governors had final authority in every matter. Until 1896 the Armenians were not given high positions in political administration. In the Congress of Berlin 'Reforms' were promised for 'the provinces inhabited by Armenians' according to which the governors in Eastern Anatolia would be accompanied by Christian assistants. The Sublime Porte did not in fact keep her promises, and the advantages conferred upon Christians were not respected fully and consistently - on the whole they remained paper promises.

In the municipal councils the Armenians were treated better, comparatively speaking. There were usually two or three of them as elected members and, in addition, the doctor or the chemist or the engineer was Armenian. Sometimes even the mayor was Armenian. It is worthy of note that the municipality was the only department of public activity where the Armenians, before and after 1896, were from time to time in the majority, probably because the municipality did not possess any political power.

ARMENIAN PARTICIPATION IN JUSTICE

The judicature was one of those fields of public life in which the Armenians were regularly represented. In the centres of the 'sancaks', especially at the provincial headquarters, there were from one to three (usually two) Armenian judges in the courts of appeal, one acting in the civil and the other in the criminal sections. In the courts of first instance, in the outlying 'kazas' one, and at the centres two Armenian members were elected. In the courts of commerce there were two or three Armenians, and in the central districts up to five. Scarcely ever were they given the post of president, normally being mere members. If we take into account the Greek participants also, it can be noticed that sometimes in the commercial courts the Christians were in the majority. Turks were not concerned much about these courts, because the trade was mostly in the hands of Greeks and Armenians, and therefore the disputes would usually involve only these two peoples. For the Turkish ruling class at that period there was a social aversion against profiting by trade.

Apart from being judges, the Armenians were admitted into the administration of justice as judicial inspectors or assistants, as 'juges d'instruction' or assistants, as executive officers, members of public prosecution committees, lawyers, notaries, clerks and process-servers.

It is interesting that, during the 'Tanzimat' period, many Armenians were employed continuously in different departments of justice. Members of the courts were elected by the people, but others were selected by the government. The motive for this behaviour was perhaps that the Turks wished to appear to patronize

their Christian subjects, or more probably because they really
needed the co-operation of qualified Armenians. We have a notable
testimony of a Turk (4) which shows the deep interest of Armenians
in law:

>As I pointed out in the last chapter, (5) among forty-five
>students of the faculty of law (at Istanbul), thirteen were
>Armenians. Thirteen out of forty-five is proportionately a large
>number, considering the small number of Armenians relatively to
>other nationalities of the Ottoman Empire. The Armenians are
>admittedly very industrious people. They won good marks in the
>entrance examination, and the authorities at the Ministry of
>Public Instruction would not affix a limit of number, but
>admitted as many as successfully passed the examination.

Not only at Istanbul, but in the universities of Syria, Europe and
the USA, Armenians studied law and, on their return home, served the
Ottoman Government. In any case the Armenian officials in the
judicature as a rule, were less in number than the Turks, since the
chairman of the judicial councils was always a Turk and there were
one or two Turkish members more than the Christians. This is one of
the reasons why the Armenians were themselves generally denied justice, in spite of the fact that many of them were included in the
courts of justice.

ARMENIAN PARTICIPATION IN FINANCE

The financial departments in the provinces of Eastern Anatolia
present the field where the Armenians had the largest participation.
They co-operated with the government in all offices of economic
affairs. The following were the special departments where they were
constantly included:

Taxation department:	about 3 Armenians
Tax collection board or Tax collection committee:	2-5 Armenians
Chamber of commerce (and agriculture):	2-5 Armenians
Ottoman Bank:	about 2 Armenians
Agricultural Bank:	about 2 Armenians
Public debt administration:	2-5 Armenians
Customs administration:	about 2 Armenians
Tobacco monopoly:	2-5 Armenians

The tobacco monopoly in the provinces was sometimes almost
entirely run by Armenian officials. Here even the administrators
were from time to time Armenian. In the taxation departments very
often the cashiers were from the Armenian community, and in the
branches of the Agricultural Bank the sole agents sometimes were
Armenian.

In public finance the posts which Armenians filled were those of
board committee member, tax collector, clerk, accountant, storekeeper, and particularly that of cashier. Evidently the Turks
trusted the Armenians in fiscal matters and employed Armenian
officials in large number. It would appear that while in connection
with political administration the Turks were very cautious, concerning financial affairs they felt quite safe towards Christian

participation. The political considerations, therefore, were one of the main factors which governed the acts of Ottomans in proportioning the offices among Muslims and Christians.

ARMENIAN PARTICIPATION IN TECHNICAL AFFAIRS AND AGRICULTURE

The technical and agricultural departments were secondary fields in which Armenian participation was not very influential or continuous. In public works Armenians were included as chief and second engineers, and as foremen, being two or three in number. They were also employed in road-making as engineers and foremen. From three to five of them worked in the provincial presses as mechanics and compositors. It is interesting to recall that in the 'vilâyets' of Sivas, Seyhan and Aleppo, the government presses had sections for Armenian printing. In the postal and telegraphic services Armenians acted as directors, operators and translators, especially in the foreign language divisions. At the centres of the 'sancaks' or provinces, Armenian participation in technical affairs was quite remarkable, but in the 'kazas' it was limited.

As for agriculture, Armenians were employed in the agricultural and forestry boards, and in the inspectorates of agriculture and forests. In each of these departments there were two or three Armenian officials, and sometimes as many as six. It was particularly common to see forestry or agricultural Armenian inspectors in various provinces of Anatolia.

ARMENIAN PARTICIPATION IN THE SECRETARIAT AND EDUCATION

In the government departments of Eastern Anatolia Armenians were mostly to be found in secretarial positions. They were employed as clerks, copyists or accountants in administrative and municipal councils, in different financial chambers, in the courts, and in technical affairs. In each office there would be two or three of them. Armenian clerks were employed in a larger number in purely secretarial work; i.e. the chief secretariat, chamber of archives, state land registry, and the investigation committees for title-deeds. Naturally there were more Armenians acting in the centres of the provinces than in the outer 'kazas'. Armenian translators were employed in the provincial headquarters as chief translators, especially in the 'vilâyets' of Van, Erzurum and Seyhan; and in the postal and telegraphic services in the foreign language sections. The translators, clerks or accountants were called to office not by election but by appointment. Why is it that relatively so many Armenians were admitted to secretarial duties? I suggest that the reason was that they were generally honest and methodical in their work; no other explanation is satisfactory.

In the field of education, two or three Armenians were included on each of the education councils and committees. The councils were established in the 'sancak' centres, and the committees in the 'kazas'. It is interesting that Tigran Amirdjanian was the head of the education council in Van, from 1893 to 1897; in Damascus Hambartzum Efendi Nizamian was the vice-director and a teacher in

the government secondary school, about 1900, and in Beirut the first
and second assistants to the director of state secondary school were
Armenian in 1893-4. Armenian teachers were employed in preparatory
and secondary schools and in the schools of arts and crafts. They
usually taught French, mathematics, science, and among various
crafts particularly carpenter's work and carpet weaving. It is
important to note that from about 1890 the Armenian language was
introduced in the syllabus of the government secondary schools in
the centres of the provinces of Diyarbakir, Erzurum, Seyhan, Elâzig
and Aleppo. Possibly it was taught also in the 'vilâyets' of Van,
Bitlis and Sivas, but no evidence on this matter was available.

It is worthy of mention that in respect of editing official
newspapers Armenians rendered a noticeable assistance to the local
governments. In Sivas Adranik Efendi Vardanian was the editor of
'Sîvâs' from 1875/6 onwards; in Diyarbakir Sahak Efendi Shishmanian
was the editor of 'Diyârbakir' about 1880, while in Aleppo the
weekly 'al-Furât' ('The Euphrates') was published in Turkish and
Arabic as well as in Armenian, one and a half years during 1286-7H/
1869-71.

ARMENIAN PARTICIPATION IN THE PUBLIC HEALTH SERVICE AND POLICE FORCE

The participation of Armenians in the department of public health of
Eastern Anatolia has been described generally as minor in comparison
with their contribution to the political administration, justice and
finance. Although their share was larger and more constant, in some
provinces and in particular periods, nevertheless it was the
Armenians who in the main carried on the medical service together
with the Turks. The Greeks were employed more in the army medical
corps and were in a predominant position only in the province of
Trebizond.

The Armenian participation in public health was remarkable in
the 'vilâyets' of Diyarbakir, Sivas, Seyhan, Elâzig and particularly
in Aleppo, Damascus and Beirut. Whereas in other places the medical
contribution of Armenians, compared with the other aspects of their
activities, was small in the latter three provinces it was of the
first rank. Armenians, who even went so far as New York to study
medicine, nostalgically preferred their native Anatolia to the
expanding New World and the prospect of lucrative practice. Armenian
medical men were employed chiefly in the local municipalities of
different districts, and also in the government hospitals at Sivas,
Seyhan, Aleppo, Damascus and Beirut. They held various posts, but
usually were doctors, surgeons and chemists; and their activity was
larger and more firmly established at the centres of the provinces
than in the 'kazas'.

In connection with the police force, Armenians were included only
in the police stations at the centres of the 'provinces inhabited by
Armenians', and scarcely ever in outer districts. They were employed as assistant superintendents of police, police sergeants, and
policemen, but were few in number.

PARTICIPATION OF GREEKS, SYRIANS AND KURDS IN OTTOMAN PUBLIC LIFE OF
EASTERN ANATOLIA AND SYRIA

It is advisable for comparative study to notice the parallel
participation of the other principal non-Turkish elements of the
population. Summing up the participation of the communities other
than Armenian, it is clear that none of them had such a large and
permanent co-operation with the Ottoman Government in the public
affairs of Eastern Anatolia and Syria as the Armenian 'millet'. The
Greeks worked in the governments of all provinces, but only in the
'vilâyet' of Trebizond, the ancient capital of the Pontine Empire
and a historic centre of Hellenism, were they more influential than
the Armenians. Generally speaking they took part in most aspects of
Ottoman public life; their contribution, however, was particularly
noticeable in the public health service and political administration. In judicature and finance also their participation was of
value, but in technical affairs, and especially in education, secretariat, agriculture and the police force, their influence was almost
negligible.
   Syrian officials in Ottoman government work were found in the
'vilâyets' of Diyarbakir, Bitlis and Van. Possibly there were some
in other provinces as well, but I was not able to identify them.
They served the departments of political administration, justice and
finance.
   As to the Kurds, I succeeded in finding personal names which are
exclusively Kurdish only in the 'vilâyets' of Bitlis and Van. They
were included in political administration, judicature and the police
force, and as far as I was able to recognize them, were very few.
We must always remember in this connection that the Kurdish community was in essence nomadic and rustic. Civilized culture was
alien to them, and all governments were obnoxious, whether Ottoman
or Persian. However, individual Kurds, once removed from their
native pastures, have achieved distinction in the Ottoman forces.
   In all the local Armenian histories of Anatolia I have not come
across any evidence that there was a rivalry between the Armenian
and other minorities in respect of their participation in public
affairs. Apparently the Christian communities lived together in
harmonious and peaceful relations.

HOW THE 'LOYAL COMMUNITY' BECAME THE 'HATED COMMUNITY' IN THE
OTTOMAN EMPIRE

The Armenians in the very early days of the conquest of
Constantinople were treated by the Ottomans in a friendly manner and
were granted all the privileges proper to a religious community
within the Ottoman and Islamic framework. Especially in the
eighteenth and nineteenth centuries, in fact until about 1875, when
many Armenian notables served the Ottoman Court as bankers, mint-
masters, superintendents of powder-mills and architects, (6) the
Armenian community was regarded and called by the Turks as 'millet-i
sadîka' ('the loyal community'). It is instructive to note how
Ubicini about 1850, speaking of the Christians of the Ottoman
Empire, said that 'the Greek and Slavonic population are

instinctively hostile', (7) while he described the Armenians as
'peaceable, industrious, and contented, connected by interest with
the Turks'. (8) But in the second half of the nineteenth century,
as the 'Tanzimat' and the new provincial organization gave to the
Armenians opportunity of participating in Ottoman public affairs on
a large scale, the Turkish-Armenian concord instead of becoming more
fraternal and tactful, descended to suspicion and antagonism. How
did this change come about? The bonds of peace and harmony between
the Turks and Armenians did not decay suddenly, but decreased in the
course of time and through unfortunate events:

(a) The first troubles, in my opinion, started with the Armenian
'National Constitution'. In 1856 when the 'Hatti hümayun' (Imperial
rescript) of the Ottoman Government promised to non-Muslim communities re-instatement of all immunities and rights in an advanced
form, the Armenians were hopeful that their civil life, particularly
in Anatolia, would be reformed and secured. They immediately com-
piled a community-regulation and presented it to the Sublime Porte.
It was rejected on the ground that 'no state can be within another
state'. (9) In this formula we see a new subtle influence: Young
European-orientated Turkish rulers began to be disillusioned with
the Islamic-Ottoman state structure. Certainly, the old Ottoman
state structure, which could readily absorb a state such as the
Republic of Ragusa and a 'nation' such as the Armenian, could
legitimately be described as 'states within a state'. Before the
days of the impingement of European ideas, it could never have
occurred to an official in the Sublime Porte to have used such an
expression. Subsequently the Armenians prepared a new constitution
(1860) which, on the suggestions of the Ottoman Government, was revised and altered in some places. The people, being very anxious to
have the new regulation, organized demonstrations, whereupon the
police intervened to establish peace, and finally on 30 March 1863
Sultan Abdül'aziz by a special Imperial rescript, ratified the new
'Regulation of the Armenian Patriarchate'.

(b) In 1878 the Armenians were involved in the negotiations of
the Treaties of San Stefano and Berlin and with the assistance of
Russia and Great Britain drew the attention of Europe to the
Armenian Question and succeeded in obtaining 'improvements and
reforms' from the Ottoman Government for the 'provinces inhabited by
Armenians'. Sultan Abdülhamid II and the Sublime Porte were angry
with this conduct of the Armenians and they did not fulfil their
promises of 'Reforms'. In desperation the Armenians protested and
demonstrated against the Government. Massive massacres were carried
out during the years 1894-6 in Anatolia and Istanbul, until under
the pressure from the Great Powers the Sublime Porte began reluc-
tantly to execute the 'Reforms'. At that time the Armenians, since
they enjoyed the protection of some European States, were suspected
of duplicity and of being agents of Great Britain and especially of
Russia. (10)

(c) After the Congress of Berlin Armenian political parties were
founded to defend the life of the Armenians in Anatolia and with the
help of Europe, to hasten the effectuation of the 'Reforms'. These
were: the Huntchakian Socialist Party, formed in Geneva in 1887,
and the Armenian Revolutionary Federation ('Hay Yeghaphokhakan
Dashnaktsuthiwn'), founded in Tiflis in 1890. The members of these

parties in Anatolia were mostly Turkish Armenians, but the founders
and leaders were from Russian Armenia, influenced by the guerilla
tactics of the Russian revolutionists. In Europe they achieved
favourable relations with English and French diplomatists and in
Istanbul they organized demonstrations demanding the execution of
the 'Reforms'. The climaxes of their audacious and imprudent
activities were the siege of the Ottoman Bank of Galata (26 August
1896) and the attempt with aid of a time-bomb on the life of the
Sultan Abdülhamid (1905) which failed and caused a new massacre.

In 1908 the Young Turks came into power and in 1909 the Sultan
was deposed, but the Armenians, for the reasons mentioned above,
were no longer regarded as 'millet-i sadîka'. The leaders of the
Young Turks and of those of the Armenian political parties were at
first of one mind and banded together, but generally speaking the
Turks were so full of suspicion and intolerance that the way was
already prepared for the 'final solution' of the Armenian Question
in the First World War.

PRINCIPAL FINDINGS

The present work enables us to give here some general conclusions on
Ottoman-Armenian relations, and particularly concerning the partici-
pation of the Armenian people in Ottoman public life in Eastern
Anatolia and Syria from 1860 to 1908.

(a) In Eastern Anatolia and Syria there lived a large Armenian
community which, according to my estimate, numbered at least
1,500,000 in the second half of the nineteenth century. They were a
civilized and hard-working people, and as such contributed much to
the economy as well as to the affairs of government there.

(b) After the new geographical-administrative division and
organization of the Ottoman Empire in 1864, a demand for many more
officials arose. The Armenians filled the necessity acting in
almost all departments. In some fields of public life their
participation was steady, as in finance, municipal councils, law
courts, the secretariat, but fluctuated in others, as in the technical field, public health and agriculture.

(c) It would appear that the political questions were an important factor in the method of the Ottoman Government in employing
Christian officials. For instance, in municipalities and in
finance departments the Armenians were included, comparatively
speaking, in considerable numbers and continuously; whereas in
administrative and judicial councils they were kept to a minority,
and as to the police force Armenians appear to have been barred from
participation. Although in the 'Reforms' of 1896 it was said that
the Christians would have policemen and 'gendarmes' in the governments according to their number, even then this promise was not
honoured. To my view, the 'Reforms' for which the Armenian
ecclesiastical and civil leaders strove so hard, instead of being
any help in reforming the life of the Armenian community in
Anatolia, were transformed into a calamity exciting the anger of
Sultan Abdülhamid and of the Turkish nationalists of the new school
who had no toleration for the autonomous 'nations' of the Ottoman
past.

(d) In spite of the unfortunate events, we notice that Armenians continued to serve the Ottoman Government. In retaining Armenian officials the Turks were in part respecting public feeling among the Christian peoples, and at the same time satisfying the European States, particularly Great Britain, France and Russia, who showed an interest in the Armenian Question. From this it follows that the Armenians performed great services for the Ottoman Government, but received little in return.

THE LETTER OF THE ARMENIAN DELEGATES SUBMITTED TO THE CONGRESS OF BERLIN

Haus-, Hof- und Staatsarchiv Wien
Politisches Archiv III, Karton 115
Berliner Kongress.

Schreiben der armenischen Delegierten
an den Minister des Aeussern, Grafen Károlyi.
Excellence!

Chargés, par S.S. le Patriarche Arménien de Constantinople et l'Assemblée nationale des Arméniens de Turquie de la mission de plaider la cause de notre peuple auprès des Puissances réunies en Congrès, nous nous adressons à Votre Excellence pour La prier de vouloir bien prendre en considération nos demandes.

Les Arménians, dont la cause sera soumise au Congrès par le fait même de l'Article 16 du Traité de St. Stefano, désirent avoir les améliorations administratives, qui seront données aux populations chrétiennes de la Turquie d'Europe, car le régime sous lequel ils ont vécu jusqu'à présent en Arménie est bien plus oppressif que celui subi par les races chrétiennes de la Turquie d'Europe.

Nous ne réclamons donc pas de liberté politique et nous ne voulons nullement nous séparer du Gouvernement Turc. Nous voulons seulement avoir dans une partie de L'Arménie Turque, c'est-à-dire dans les 'vilâyets' d'Erzeroum et de Van et dans la partie septentrionale du 'vilâyet' de Diarbekir (v. la carte ci-jointe) où nous avons la majorité sur les Turcs, conformément aux documents statistiques ci-inclus, nous voulons avoir, disons nous, un 'vali' arménien nommé par la S. Porte avec l'assentiment des Puissances. Ce 'vali' sera chargé de l'administration locale pour un temps déterminé; il devra disposer d'une police pour maintenir l'ordre et la sécurité, et d'une partie des revenus du pays, pour en assurer le développement moral et matériel.

Le Projet de Réglement organique que nous avons l'honneur de soumettre à l'appréciation de Votre Excellence aussi bien qu'à celle de tous les Plénipotentiaires, pourra donner à Votre Excellence une idée sur le caractère et les détails du régime administratif, que nous sollicitons aujourd'hui pour la paix et le bien être des populations de l'Arménie Turque.

Notre expérience personelle des hommes et des choses de l'Orient nous porte à prendre la liberté de déclarer qu'un Gouverneur Turc et

une administration musulmane ne peuvent pas faire les réformes
nécessaires à notre pays. Si le Gouvernement Turc est laissé libre
dans le choix du 'vali' arménien, les caprices de Constantinople
perpétueraient fatalement les abus mêmes que l'Europe cherche à
faire disparaitre. S'il conserve le droit de changer le 'vali'
arbitrairement, il ne lui laissera ni le temps de consolider son
autorité, ni celui d'entreprendre des réformes nécessaires et
sérieuses. Si c'est au Gouvernement Turc à élire les fonctionnaires
du 'vilâyet', il tombera dans les mêmes erreurs que par le passé.
Si le 'vali' n'a pas une gendarmerie sous ses ordres, son autorité
sera tout-à-fait impuissante. Si on laisse au Gouvernement central
la faculté de régler lui-même le budget de la Province, il
s'emparerait de tous les revenus, ne laissant au pays qu'une somme
si minime, que tout progrès et toute bonne administration
deviendraient impossibles. Si enfin tous ces arrangments n'étaient
pas sauvegardés par la garantie d'une surveillance européenne, les
tristes traditions du régime musulman feraient nécessairement
renaître ces convulsions periodiques que les efforts de l'Europe
réunie cherchent à prévenir.

Après ces explications succinctes, nous avons l'honneur de
soumettre notre cause à la sagesse et à l'équité de Votre Excellence
en La priant de vouloir bien lui accorder son bien veillant appui au
sein du Congrès.

Veuillez agréer, Excellence, l'hommage de notre plus haute
considération.

Délégués des Arméniens de Turquie:
Berlin, le 25 juin 1878.   Khorène de Nar Bey
                                            Archévêque de Beschiktasch
(Signé: Meguerditch Kherimian, Archévêque de Daron et ex-Patriarche
         des Arméniens de Turquie.)

A MODERN TURK ON THE ARMENIAN PAST

Günay Erinal (Assistant to the Agricultural Inspector), 'Fabrika
yemi' (Manufactured Animal Food), 'Milliyet', Istanbul, 25 October
1962, translated by M.K.K.

There is a famine in Eastern Turkey. Last winter all the newspapers
reported that animals were dying of hunger. Bulanik is a 'kaza'
which is also suffering from lack of animal food in the East. The
local bank offered to give food to the peasants' animals. In
looking through the documents I noticed the following letter:
   We do not approve of manufactured food which the bank is offering
   to give us. Instead of food we want to be given money.
Why did they refuse the offer of the bank? Is it because they did
not know what factory food was, or because they did not need any?
The first suggestion is much more likely. In the beginning of 1962
in Saimbeyli (Haçin) the villagers said:
   In the days of the Armenians more people lived here; the grapes
   and their wine were very well known. At that time there was also
   a college, which disappeared with the Armenians. 'The making of
   wine is sinful', we said, and destroyed the vineyards. In course
   of time Saimbeyli was deserted by most of its inhabitants. In
   the old houses of the Armenians the wine cellars still remain.
'In the days of the Armenians here ....' I had heard these words
long ago, and I heard them very often recently. In July 1961 we
were listening to the radio in the one-roomed house of Dr Enver
Dagaşan. At night there was a knock on the door and we saw a
'gendarme':
   'Doctor Bey', he said, 'the villages of Hunu and Lorşun have
   quarrelled and fired on each other. It is necessary to
   intervene.'
The 'kaymakam', the superintendent of police, the doctor and the
'gendarmerie' commandant sat in a car and went to Hunu. The next
day I found out the reason for the dispute between the two villages.
Through Hunu flows a stream called Hunu Çayi. A tributary of this
stream flows into Lorşun. The people of Hunu, claiming that their
water was not enough, damned the branch of Lorşun. The 'kaymakam'
went and ordered that Lorşun must have water two days a week,
putting a 'gendarme' on the border. The people of Hunu again

stopped the water, whereupon an armed fight, like an open battle, took place.

This stream has been a point of dispute between Afşin and Elbistan as well. When I was there, two committees from the two 'kazas' were discussing an agreement in the presence of the 'kaymakam'. I do not know the result, because meanwhile I went somewhere else. At that time some people said:

When the Armenians were here there was a dam on the river by virtue of which we had no shortage of water. Parts of this barrage still remain in the water, and three or four hundred sacks of cement would be more than enough to repair the dam.

If the two villages come together and accomplish this work, then both 'kazas' of Afşin and Elbistan may have sufficient water.

In Hakkâri also I heard Armenians mentioned. The valley of Zap runs from Hakkâri to Çukurca through rocky mountains. The officer of the bank, who was from Hakkâri itself and named Coşkun, said:

'The Armenians, by planting terrace-vineyards on the steep mountain-side, produced grapes, and it was very successful.'

'But it does not exist now', I said.

'Our people neglected the land', he added.

In the Gürpinar 'kaza' of Van there is a spring of the same name. Two streams come out of this spring; one flows towards Van and into the lake near Edremit, and the other flows in the opposite direction through the plains. The length of the first stream is said to be more than 70 km, but I do not know about the second, probably it is longer. These were also set in order by Armenians, and now both of them are abandoned. The water is being exploited, but not as efficiently as by the Armenians.

In the Çatak 'kaza' of Van there are thousands of pistachio nut trees, but they are not fertile. Last year some trees were fertile, but this year the new shoots were not pruned, due to the lack of skilled gardeners. On the road to Hakkâri and on the boundaries of the Zap valley there are infertile pistachio nut trees. As yet nobody has looked after them, in spite of the fact that the value of the pistachio nut is well known.

I knew Eastern Turkey from what had remained in my memory from the geography books which we had learned at school: mountainous, stony, rocky, with long-lasting winters and summers so short that one may say they hardly come. I saw uncultivated land there. Between Adilcavaz and Van, Van and Hakkâri there are many such places. You might have said that 'They breed cattle and produce grass there.' There was no grass to reap, and as far as my eye could reach I did not see a single animal. In my opinion this means that, apart from their ignorance, our peasants also do not like to work, though it would be very easy to make these people profitable.

NOTES

INTRODUCTION

1   The text of this Imperial rescript can be found in 'Dûstûr'
    ('Code of Laws'), Istanbul, vol.1, 1289H/1872-3, pp.7-14.   In
    French translation see G. Young, 'Corps de droit ottoman', vol.
    2, pp.3-9;   E. Engelhardt, 'La Turquie et le Tanzimat ou
    histoire des réformes dans l'Empire Ottoman depuis 1826 jusqu'à
    nos jours', vol.1, pp.263-70;   and G. Noradounghian, 'Recueil
    d'actes internationaux de l'Empire Ottoman', vol.3, pp.83-8.
2   P. Ketchian, 'Patmuthiwn surb Perktchi hiwandanotsin Hayots i
    Kostandnupolis' ('History of St Perkitch Hospital of the
    Armenians in Constantinople'), p.95.
3   This Constitution was edited by A. Berberian, in his 'Patmuthiwn
    Hayots' ('History of the Armenians'), pp.390-427.
4   The revised Constitution was drafted and published by the
    Armenian Patriarchate at Istanbul in 1863, which contains both
    the Armenian and Turkish (in Armenian characters) texts in
    parallel lines, 'Azgayin Sahmanadruthiwn Hayots' ('National
    Constitution of the Armenians').   The Turkish official version
    was published in the Ottoman 'Dûstûr' ('Code of Laws'),
    Istanbul, vol.2, 1289H/1872-3, pp.938-61.   In this the 'Preface'
    and the 'Fundamental principles' are omitted (see the Armenian
    text, pp.9-12).   An English translation of the Constitution was
    published by H.F.B. Lynch, in his 'Armenia: Travels and
    Studies', vol.2, pp.445-67.   There is an abridged French
    translation by Young, in his 'Corps de droit ottoman', vol.2,
    pp.79-92.
5   See 'Dûstûr' ('Code of Laws'), vol.2, p.6 (the index).
    Curiously enough the text itself (p.938) has no title.
6   'Millet' is an Arabic word, 'millah', whose original meaning in
    the classical literature was 'a religion, a way of belief and
    practice in respect of religion', E.W. Lane, 'An Arabic-English
    Lexicon', 2nd imp., USA, 1955-6, book 8 and supplement, p.3023.
    Cf. 'EI', 1st edn, vol.3, pp.497-8.   In modern Arabic, in
    addition to its old sense, it came to mean also a religious
    community, H. Wehr, 'A Dictionary of Modern Written Arabic', ed.
    J.M. Cowan, Wiesbaden, 1961, p.918, whence in Turkish 'millet' =

'community, people united in a common faith'.

7 'Teghekagirq gawarakan harstaharutheants' ('Report on the Outrages which Occurred in the Provinces'), Istanbul, 1876.

8 A. Sarukhan, 'Haykakan khendir ew Azgayin Sahmanadruthiwń
   Turqiayum' ('The Armenian Question and the National Constitution
   in Turkey'), p.285.

9 E. Hertslet, 'The Map of Europe by Treaty', vol.4, p.2686;
   T.E. Holland, 'The European Concert in the Eastern Question',
   p.343, and G. Noradounghian, 'Recueil d'actes internationaux de
   l'Empire Ottoman', vol.3, p.516 (the full text pp.507-21).

10 PRO - FO, 78/1521, pp.12-13.

11 The Marquis of Salisbury to Her Majesty's Embassies, 1 April
   1878, 'British and Foreign State Papers 1877-1878', vol.69,
   1885, pp.812-13.

12 Haus-, Hof- und Staatsarchiv Wien, Politisches Archiv iii,
   Karton 115, 'Berliner Kongress', the letter, Schreiben der
   armenischen Delegierten an den Minister des Aeussern, Grafen
   Károlyi, dated 25 June 1878. It is signed only by the two
   clergymen. See Appendix 1.

13 Hertslet, 'The Map of Europe by Treaty', vol.4, p.2796.

14 See Kherimian's 'Literary Collection' (in Armenian),
   p.98; H. Adjemian, 'Hayots Hayrik' ('Armenians' Father'),
   vol.2, pp.511-14, and 'Mshak' ('Cultivator', a newspaper), 1878,
   no.159.

15 'The Times', 20 November 1894, p.11c.

16 'The Times', 28 December 1897, p.2d.

17 'The Times', 21 November 1894, p.5; 25 December 1894, p.3c;
   26 December 1894, p.3c, and 21 January 1895, p.5d.

18 M. Jewett, United States Consul at Sivas, was to present a
   separate report on the Armenian troubles to the General
   Secretary of the States, see 'The Times', 8 December 1894, p.5a.

19 Noradounghian, 'Recueil d'actes internationaux de l'Empire
   Ottoman', vol.4, 1903, pp.511-19; Young, 'Corps de droit
   ottoman', vol.1, pp.97-105; A. Schopoff, 'Les Réformes et la
   protection des chrétiens en Turquie 1673-1904', pp.518-25, and
   M. Léart (K. Zohrap), 'La Question Arménienne à la lumière des
   documents', pp.53-8.

20 See E.Z. Karal, 'Osmanli tarihi' ('Ottoman History'), vol.7
   (1861-76), pp.152ff.

CHAPTER 1 THE ARMENIANS OF DIYARBAKIR

1 Strabo's 'Geography', xi, 14, 15 and xii, 2.9; Tacitus, 'The
   Annals', xiv, 23-5 and xv, 3-5; Plutarch, 'Lucullus' in the
   'Lives', vol.3, pp.259-61, 275 and 286-7; C.F. Lehmann-Haupt,
   'Armenien einst und jetzt', vol.1, pp.381-429 and 501-23; Y.
   Manandian, 'Hayastani glkhawor djanaparhnere' ('The Main Routes
   of Armenia'), pp.85-114, and idem, 'Tigran II ew Hrome' ('Tigran
   II and Rome'), pp.61-72.

2 'CTA', vol.2, p.412.

3 The official name of the Armenian national Church is 'The Holy
   Apostolic and Orthodox Church of Armenia'. The majority of
   Armenians (85 per cent) are members of this Church, and they

prefer to be called 'Apostolic' rather than 'Orthodox' or 'Gregorian'. Cuinet, as well as some other European and Turkish authors refer to the members of the Apostolic Church as 'Gregorian', after the name of the Illuminator of Armenia, St Gregory, but I have used the term 'Apostolic', because the Armenians received their Christian faith before St Gregory through the Apostles Thaddaeus and Bartholomew.

4   A. Cevâd, Diyar Bakr in his 'Memâliki osmâniyenin târîkh ve cogrâfyâ lugâti' ('Historical and Geographical Dictionary of the Ottoman Empire'), vol.2, p.402, presents the total of the Armenian population of Diyarbakir as 57,196 which is even less than the figure given by Cuinet.

5   M.A., 'Turqiayi Hayern ew irents dratsiner' ('The Armenians of Turkey and their Neighbours'), see the statistical table.

6   Theodik, 'Amênun taretsoytse' ('The Almanac for Everyone'), 1922, p.261.

7   M. Léart, 'La Question Arménienne à la lumière des documents', pp.60-1, and J. Bryce, 'The Treatment of Armenians in the Ottoman Empire', p.661.

8   J. Lepsius, 'Der Todesgang des armenischen Volkes', p.74. The same author (ibid., pp.306-7) records the number of the Armenians in the province of Diyarbakir as 81,700 (Apostolic 78,000; Catholic 1,500 and Protestant 2,200) probably quoting the figures of M. Ormanian, 'The Church of Armenia', p.206.

9   N. Akinian, 'Simeon dpri Lehatswoy ughegruthiwne' ('The Travel Diary of the Scribe Simeon from Lwow'), p.205.

10 B. Nathanian, 'Artosr Hayastani' ('The Tears of Armenia'), p.58.

CHAPTER 2   THE ARMENIANS OF BITLIS

1   In the nineteenth century the 'sancak' of Bingöl was called Genç. Now under the name of Genç exists only a 'kaza'.

2   The Syrians of Bitlis were Armenian-speaking, according to the eye-witness account of Lynch: 'They [the Syrians] speak Armenian and are familiar with Turkish. The Bible is expounded to them in Armenian, which may be said to be their native tongue' ('Armenia: Travels and Studies', vol.2, p.152).

3   51,500 of the Armenians lived in the 'sancak' of Bitlis; 94,000 in the 'sancak' of Muş and Bingöl; 25,000 in Siirt, and 25,000 in the 'kaza' of Hizan. M. Ormanian, 'The Church of Armenia', pp.206 and 208.

4   J. Lepsius, 'Der Todesgang des armenischen Volkes', pp.306-7.

5   M. Léart, 'La Question Arménienne à la lumière des documents', pp.60-1, and J. Bryce, 'The Treatment of Armenians in the Ottoman Empire', p.661.

6   Theodik, 'Amênun taretsoytse' ('The Almanac for Everyone'), 1922, pp.261-2.

7   M.A., 'Turqiayi Hayern ew irents dratsiner' ('The Armenians of Turkey and their Neighbours'), see the statistical table.

8   These nomadic tribes were mostly Kurds and therefore they could be added to the Kurdish total.

9   A. Dô, 'Vani, Bitlisi ew Erzurumi vilayetnere' ('The "vilâyets" of Van, Bitlis and Erzurum'), p.83. Cf. S. Ephrikian,

'Bnashkharhik bararan' ('Armenian Geographical Dictionary'),
vol.1, p.381, and M.K. Mirakhorian, 'Nkaragrakan ugheworuthiwn i
hayabnak gawars arewelean Tadjkastani' ('Descriptive Travel in
the Provinces inhabited by Armenians in Eastern Turkey'), vol.1,
p.57.
10 H.F.B. Lynch, 'Armenia: Travels and Studies', vol.2, p.172.
Cf. A. Dô, op. cit., pp.110-11.

CHAPTER 3 THE ARMENIANS OF VAN

1 PRO - FO, 78/1682, 'Tabular View of the Population of the
"mutasarriflik" of Wan'. Included in these figures are the
following: the city of Van: Christians 10,000, Muslims 8,000.
Neighbourhood of the city: Christians 32,000, Muslims 9,000.
2 'CTA', vol.2, p.636, cf. A. Cevâd, 'Memâliki osmâniyenin târîkh
ve cogrâfyâ lugâti' ('Historical and Geographical Dictionary of
the Ottoman Empire'), vol.3, p.830, and Ş. Fraşerî, 'Qâmûs
ül-a'lâm' ('Dictionary of Proper Names'), vol.4, p.4673.
3 PRO - FO, 78/2439, 'Consul Taylor's report on Koordistan' (18
March 1869), cf. H.F.B. Lynch, 'Armenia: Travels and Studies',
vol.2, p.79.
4 M.A., 'Turqiayi Hayern ew irents dratsiner' ('The Armenians of
Turkey and their Neighbours'), see statistical table.
5 M. Ormanian, 'The Church of Armenia', pp.206 and 208; J.
Lepsius, 'Der Todesgang des armenischen Volkes', pp.76-7 and
306-7.
6 Theodik, 'Amênun taretsoytse' ('The Almanac for Everyone'),
1922, p.262.
7 H. Eramian, 'Yushartzan Van-Vaspurakani' ('Memorial of Van-
Vaspurakan'), vol.1, p.15.
8 M. Léart, 'La Question Arménienne à la lumière des documents',
pp.60-1, and J. Bryce, 'The Treatment of Armenians in the
Ottoman Empire', p.661.
9 A. Dô, 'Vani, Bitlisi ew Erzurumi vilayetnere' ('The "vilâyets"
of Van, Bitlis and Erzurum'), p.18.
10 H.F.B. Lynch, 'Armenia: Travels and Studies', vol.2, pp.83 and
89.

CHAPTER 4 THE ARMENIANS OF ERZURUM

1 PRO - FO, 78/1669, 'Report on the "eyalet" of Erzurum', No.9
(28 February 1862).
2 PRO - FO, 78/2439, 'Consul Taylor's report on Koordistan' (18
March 1869).
3 Ş. Fraşerî, 'Qâmûs ül-a'lâm' ('Dictionary of Proper Names'),
vol.2, p.830.
4 'CTA', vol.1, p.136. See the same in Cevâd's 'Memâliki
osmâniyenin târîkh ve cogrâfyâ lugâti' ('Historical and
Geographical Dictionary of the Ottoman Empire'), vol.1, p.57.
Cf. J. Lepsius, 'Der Todesgang des armenischen Volkes', p.34,
where he also gives a total for the general population of the
province as 645,700.

5 M. Léart, 'La Question Arménienne à la lumière des documents',
   pp.60-1; J. Bryce, 'The Treatment of Armenians in the Ottoman
   Empire', p.661; Theodik, 'Amênun taretsoytse' ('The Almanac for
   Everyone'), 1922, p.261.
6 M. Ormanian, 'The Church of Armenia', pp.205-6; J. Lepsius,
   'Der Todesgang des armenischen Volkes', pp.304-5.
7 R. Dalyell in PRO - FO, 78/1669, report No.9 (1862).
8 A. Dô, 'Vani, Bitlisi ew Erzurumi vilâyetnere' ('The "vilâyets"
   of Van, Bitlis and Erzurum'), p.163.
9 'CTA', vol.1, p.137.
10 'CTA', vol.1, p.136.

CHAPTER 5 THE ARMENIANS OF TREBIZOND

1 Ghevond Vardapet, 'Arshawanq Arabats i Hays' ('The Invasions of
   Arabs into Armenia'), pp.201-3; S. Taronetsi, 'Patmuthiwn
   tiezerakan' ('General History'), p.134; M. Ormanian,
   'Azgapatum' ('History of the Armenian Nation'), vol.1, pp.900-2,
   and V. Minorsky, article Laz, 'EI', 1st edn, vol.3, p.21.
2 M. Bejishkian, 'Patmuthiwn Pontosi' ('History of Pontus'), p.97;
   Y. Dashian, 'Hay bnaktchuthiwne Sew Dzovên mintchew Karin' ('The
   Armenian Population from Black Sea to Karin'), pp.31-2; S.
   Ephrikian, 'Bnashkharhik bararan' ('Armenian Geographical
   Dictionary'), vol.2, article Lazistan, pp.82-3, and H. Adjarian,
   'Qnnuthiwn Hamsheni barbari' ('Study of the Dialect of
   Hamshen').
3 'CTA', vol.1, p.10, cf. A. Cevâd, 'Memâliki osmâniyenin târîkh
   ve cogrâfyâ lugâti' ('Historical and Geographical Dictionary of
   the Ottoman Empire'), vol.2, p.522.
4 In the 'sancak' of Trebizond: 21,435; Samsun: 18,465;
   Gümüşane: 2,200 and Rize: 5,100.
5 The Laz are of South Caucasian stock. Their native tongue is
   Mingrelian. They were Christians since the seventh century, but
   after the Ottoman conquest of Trebizond, they were converted to
   Islam.
6 Ş. Fraşerî, 'Qâmûs ül-a'lâm' ('Dictionary of Proper Names'),
   vol.4, p.3005.
7 'Tarabzon vilâyeti salnamesi', 1320H/1902-3, pp.338-9. In the
   provincial year-books of 1321H/1903-4 (pp.470-3) and of 1322H/
   1904-5 (pp.430-3), the total of the Armenians is given as
   51,639.
8 Theodik, 'Amênun taretsoytse' ('The Almanac for Everyone'),
   1922, p.262.
9 M. Ormanian, 'The Church of Armenia', p.205; J. Lepsius, 'Der
   Todesgang des armenischen Volkes', pp.304-5.
10 'CTA', vol.1, pp.10 and 120, and Ephrikian, op. cit., pp.532-3.

CHAPTER 6 THE ARMENIANS OF SIVAS

1 G. Cedrenus, 'Annales' (I. Bekker's edition), vol.2, p.464; S.
   Anetsi, 'Hawaqmunq i grots patmagrats' ('A Collection from
   History Books'), pp.104-5; Vardan Vardapet, 'Hawaqumn

patmuthean' ('A Historical Collection'), p.92, and Th. Ardzruni, 'Patmuthiwn tann Ardzruneats' ('History of the Ardzruni Dynasty'), pp.499-500. This last historian records the number of Armenian immigrants to Sivas as '14,000 men, not including women and children'. M. Tchamtchian, 'Patmuthiwn Hayots' ('History of the Armenians'), vol.2, p.903, gives the number as 400,000 people, while Minorsky (art. Wân, 'EI', 1st edn, vol.4, p.1119), as 40,000 families.

2 'CTA', vol.1, pp.617-18.
3 Ş. Fraşerî, 'Qâmûs ül-a'lâm' ('Dictionary of Proper Names'), art. Sîvâs, vol.4, p.2797.
4 K. Gabikian, 'Eghernapatum Phoqun Hayots ew norin medzi mayraqaghaqin Sebastioy' ('History of the Massacres of Lesser Armenia and of its Great Capital Sivas'), pp.597 and 598-604.
5 Theodik, 'Amênun taretsoytse' ('The Almanac for Everyone'), 1922, p.261.
6 M. Ormanian, 'The Church of Armenia', pp.205 and 207; cf. J. Lepsius, 'Der Todesgang des armenischen Volkes', pp.304-7.
7 B. Nathanian, 'Teghekagruthiwn endhanur vidjakin Sebastioy' ('Report on the General Diocese of Sivas'), pp.148-9.
8 'CTA', vol.1, p.620.
9 A. Alboyadjian, 'Patmuthiwn Eudokioy Hayots' ('History of the Armenians in Tokat'), pp.1298, 1305-6 (see also p.1298).
10 Nathanian, op. cit., pp.67-8.

CHAPTER 7 THE ARMENIANS OF SEYHAN

1 J. Garstang and O.R. Gurney, 'The Geography of the Hittite Empire', pp.60-1.
2 Concerning the life of Philaretos see M. Urhayetsi, 'Jamanakagruthiwn' ('The Chronicles of Matthew from Urha'), pp. 206-34; Vardan Vardapet, 'Hawaqumn patmuthean' ('A Historical Collection'), pp.104-7; K. Gantzaketsi, 'Patmuthiwn Hayots' ('History of the Armenians'), p.78; Michael of Syria, 'Chronicles' (in Armenian), p.399; J. Laurent, Byzance et Antioche sous le curopalate Philarète, 'Revue des Études Arméniennes', vol.9, 1929, pp.61-72; Kommagenatsi (E. Kassuni), 'Philartos Haye' ('Philaretos the Armenian'), and R. Grousset, 'L'Empire du Levant', 2nd edn, pp.176-85.
3 Gregor of Akants, 'History of the Nation of the Archers' (translated from the Armenian by R.P. Blake and R.N. Frye), pp. 73 and 75; Gantzaketsi, op. cit., pp.350-7; Vardan Vardapet, op. cit., pp.148-9, and Grousset, op. cit., pp.397-8.
4 An accurate history of the Armenian kingdom of Cilicia is by G.G. Michayelian, 'Istoria Kilikiyskovo Armianskovo gosudarstva' ('History of the Armenian State of Cilicia').
5 'CTA', vol.2, p.5, cf. A. Cevâd, 'Memâliki osmâniyenin târîkh ve cogrâfyâ lugâti' ('Historical and Geographical Dictionary of the Ottoman Empire'), art. Atana, vol.1, p.15.
6 Ş. Fraşerî, 'Qâmûs ül-a'lâm' ('Dictionary of Proper Names'), art. Atana, vol.1, p.219.
7 M. Ormanian, 'The Church of Armenia', p.207.
8 J. Lepsius, 'Der Todesgang des armenischen Volkes', pp.304-5.

9   Theodik, 'Amênun taretsoytse' ('The Almanac for Everyone'),
    1922, p.262.
10 S. Ephrikian, 'Bnashkharhik bararan' ('Armenian Geographical
    Dictionary'), vol.1, p.272. Concerning the occupation of
    Armenians in trades and crafts in Sis, see M. Keleshian, 'Sis-
    matean' ('A Book on Sis'), pp.423–32, and for Saimbeyli, see
    Y.P. Boghosian, 'Hadjini endhanur patmuthiwn' ('The General
    History of Haçin'), pp.165–76.

CHAPTER 8 THE ARMENIANS OF ELÂZIG

1   V. Minorsky, art. Ma'mûret al-'Azîz, 'EI', 1st edn, vol.3, p.
    224; J. Kramers, art. Kharpût, 'EI', 1st edn, vol.2, pp.915–16;
    B. Darkot, art. El'aziz, 'IA', fascicle 31,
    pp.221–2; 'CTA', vol.2, p.317, and the year-books of the pro-
    vince of Ma'mûret ül-'Azîz.
2   52,407 Armenians lived in the 'sancak' of Elâzig; 9,933 in
    Malatya, and 13,076 in Hozat.
3   'CTA', vol.2, p.322.
4   Theodik, 'Amênun taretsoytse' ('The Almanac for Everyone'),
    1922, p.261.
5   M. Ormanian, 'The Church of Armenia', pp.206–7; J. Lepsius,
    'Der Todesgang des armenischen Volkes', pp.306–7.
6   V. Hayk (Haig), 'Kharpert ew anor oskeghên dashte' ('Harput and
    her Golden Plain'), p.53.
7   S. Ephrikian, 'Bnashkharhik bararan' ('Armenian Geographical
    Dictionary'), vol.2, p.161.
8   Nathanian, 'Artosr Hayastani' ('The Tears of Armenia'), p.136.
9   M. Barsamian, 'Akn ew Aknetsiq' ('Egin and its Armenian
    Population'), p.144.
10 A. Alboyadjian, 'Patmuthiwn Malatioy Hayots' ('History of the
    Armenians in Malatya'), p.1004.

CHAPTER 9 THE ARMENIANS OF SYRIA I. THE PROVINCE OF ALEPPO

1   A. Sürmeyan, 'Mayr tsutsak hayerên tzeragrats Jerusalemi srbots
    Yakobeants vanqi' ('Catalogue of the Armenian Manuscripts of St
    James's Monastery in Jerusalem'), vol.1, pp.347–8; idem,
    'Patmuthiwn Halepi Hayots' ('History of the Armenians of
    Aleppo'), pp.8–10.
2   B. Sarkisian, 'Mayr tsutsak hayerên tzeragrats matenadaranin
    Mkhithareants i Venedig' ('Catalogue of the Armenian Manuscripts
    of the Mkhitharist Library in Venice'), pp.401–2, and Sürmeyan,
    'History of the Armenians of Aleppo', pp.20–1.
3   'Haleb vilâyeti salnamesi' ('Year-book of the Province of
    Aleppo'), 1326H/1908, p.504.
4   The year-book records for all Protestants of the province of
    Aleppo as '12,071'. I have reduced this total to the half in
    order to give the approximate number of Armenian Protestants in
    this province. M. Ormanian, 'The Church of Armenia', pp.206–7,
    estimates the Armenian Protestants of Aleppo as 12,300.
5   Ormanian in ibid.; J. Lepsius, 'Der Todesgang des armenischen

Volkes', pp.304-5.
6   Theodik, 'Amênun taretsoytse' ('The Almanac for Everyone'),
    1922, pp.262-3.
7   PRO - FO, 78/1538, T.H. Skene, British Consul at Aleppo, to Home
    Office (to Sir Henry L. Bulwer), No.27, Aleppo, 4 August 1860.
8   Sürmeyan, 'History of the Armenians of Aleppo', p.973; cf.
    ibid., pp.974-8, and Gabikian, 'History of the Massacres of
    Lesser Armenia and of its Great Capital Sivas', pp.542-3.
9   J.L. Farley, 'The Resources of Turkey', p.249. See also K.H.
    Calustian, 'Marash kam Germanik ew heros Zeytun' ('Marash or
    Germanicia and the Heroic Zeytun'), pp.276-306.
10 Ph. di Tarrâzî, 'Târîkh assahâfa'l 'arabiyyah' ('History of the
    Arabic Press'), vol.1, p.68 and vol.2, pp.222-3; A. Mrueh,
    'Assahâfa'l 'arabiyyah' ('The Arabic Press'), p.207.

CHAPTER 10 THE ARMENIANS OF SYRIA II. DAMASCUS, BEIRUT AND MOUNT
LEBANON

1   On the massacres of Lebanon: I. b. Yakub Abkarius (an
    Armenian), 'The Lebanon in Turmoil: Syria and the Powers in
    1860', trans. and annotated by J.F. Scheltema; PRO - FO,
    78/1521, 'Disturbances in Syria (Mount Lebanon)'; FO, 78/1557,
    'MS Correspondence on Affairs of Syria (Disturbances), laid
    before Parliament (No.628, 1860)', which are letters and reports
    of the British consuls of Beirut, Sayda and Jerusalem, and
    'Parliamentary Papers', 1861, vol.2, 'Syria'.
2   The monastery of Bzommar was founded in 1749 and completed in
    1771, but the friars started to inhabit it in 1750. In 1923-4
    the last few friars of the order of St Anton joined the
    monastery of Bzommar.
3   M. Ormanian, 'The Church of Armenia', p.207; J. Lepsius, 'Der
    Todesgang des armenischen Volkes', pp.308-9.
4   V. Cuinet, 'Syrie, Liban et Palestine', pp.307, 386, 394, 458
    and 480. According to him 1,925 (1,025 Protestant and 900
    Apostolic) Armenians lived in the 'sancak' of Damascus, and 200
    Apostolics in Jabal al-Drûz.
5   Ormanian in ibid.; 'Beyrut vilâyeti salnamesi' ('Year-book of
    the Province of Beirut'), 1326H/1908, straight after p.424.
    According to Cuinet (op. cit., pp.14, 52, 53, 82, 89, 149, 160
    and 162) 2,931 Armenians lived in the province of Beirut about
    1895: 2,001 Apostolics (200 in Beirut, 201 in Merdj 'Ayûn and
    1,600 in Lâdhikiyya), and 930 Catholics (400 in Beirut and 530
    in Sur). These figures are higher than the numbers given by
    both the Turkish and Armenian sources.
6   Ormanian, op. cit.; Lepsius, op. cit.
7   Theodik, 'Amênun taretsoytse' ('The Almanac for Everyone'),
    1922, p.263.
8   S. Ephrikian, 'Bnashkharhik bararan' ('Armenian Geographical
    Dictionary'), vol.1, p.574.
9   S. Varjapetian, 'Hayere Libanani mêtch' ('The Armenians in
    Lebanon'), p.285.
10 Ş. Fraşerî, 'Qâmûs ül-a'lâm' ('Dictionary of Proper Names'),
    vol.3, p.2111; 'EI', 1st edn, vol.1, p.929; K.S. Salibi, art.

Dâwûd Pasha in 'EI', 2nd edn, vol.2, pp.184-5; 'IA', vol.3, p.498; State Archives of Vienna, 'Administrative Registratur des kaiserlich-königlichen Ministeriums des Aeusseren', F/9, Türkei-Wien, Karton 7, eight documents concerning Davud Pasha, dated May-June-July 1856, and two others from September 1859 (all of them published by M.K. Krikorian in 'Handês Amsoreay', Vienna, April-June 1968, pp.229-42); H.H. Jessup, 'Fifty-three Years in Syria', vol.1, pp.234, 249, 250, 254, 266-7, 290-1 and 332; Ph. Hitti, 'Lebanon in History', pp.443-5, and E. Boghosian, 'Karapet Artin Pasha Davudian, 1816-1873' (in Armenian).

CONCLUSIONS

1 'Teghekagirq gawarakan harstaharutheants' ('Report on the Outrages which Occurred in the Provinces'), Istanbul, 1876.
2 PRO - FO, 78/1538, T.H. Skene, British Consul at Aleppo, to the Home Office, No.27, Aleppo, 4 August 1860.
3 PRO - FO, 78/1588, a descriptive memorandum prepared by 'a Prussian gentleman' residing in Erzurum and sent by Consul R.A.O. Dalyell to the FO, 13 June 1861.
4 H. Halid, 'The Diary of a Turk', p.126.
5 Ibid., p.103 where it is said: 'In our first year's class at the law college, in which there were about forty-five students, the number of Armenians alone reached thirteen.'
6 M.A. Ubicini, 'Letters on Turkey', vol.2, pp.310-18; J. Deny, art. Armîniya in 'EI', 2nd edn, vol.1, p.640, and F. Nansen, 'L'Arménie et le Proche Orient', pp.297-9.
7 Ubicini, op. cit., vol.2, pp.244-5.
8 Ibid., pp.252-3.
9 P. Ketchian, 'Patmuthiwn surb Perktchi hiwandanotsin Hayots i Kostandnupolis' ('History of St Perkitch Hospital of the Armenians in Constantinople'), p.95.
10 M. Fuat Köprülü, 'Les minorités en Turquie', pp.118-21, and Halid, op. cit., pp.115-16.

BIBLIOGRAPHY

MANUSCRIPT SOURCES

AUSTRIAN ARCHIVES. Haus-, Hof- und Staatsarchiv Wien, Politisches Archiv III, Karton 115, Berliner Kongress, the letter 'Schreiben der armenischen Delegierten an den Minister des Aeussern Grafen Károlyi' (25 June 1878).
Haus-, Hof- und Staatsarchiv Wien, Administrative Registratur des kaiserlich-königlichen Ministerium des Aeussern, F/9 Türkei-Wien, Karton 7, eight documents concerning Davud Paşa, dated May–June–July 1856, and two others from September 1859 (all of them edited by M.K. Krikorian, 'Handês Amsoreay', April–June 1968).
BRITISH GOVERNMENT. 'Disturbances in Syria (Mount Lebanon)', PRO – FO, 78/1521, and 'MS correspondence on Affairs of Syria (Disturbances), laid before the Parliament (No.628, 1860)', PRO – FO, 78/1557. These are letters and reports of the British Consuls of Beirut, Sayda and Jerusalem.
DALYELL, R.A.O. (British Consul). 'Report on the "eyalet" of Erzurum, No.9 (28 February 1862)', PRO – FO, 78/1669; 'Tabular View of the Population of the "mutasarriflik" of Wan', PRO – FO, 78/1682.
OTTOMAN GOVERNMENT. 'Résumé de différents mémoires spéciaux concernant notre arrangement defensif au théâtre de la guerre arménienne', which is the report of the meetings of an assembly (1858-60), held under the presidency of Selîm Paşa, PRO – FO, 78/1521.
'PRUSSIAN GENTLEMAN'. Descriptive memorandum prepared by 'a Prussian Gentleman' residing in Erzurum and sent by British Consul R.A.O. Dalyell to the FO, 13 June 1861, PRO – FO, 78/1588.
SKENE, T.H. (British Consul). Report to the Home Office (to Sir Henry L. Bulwer), No.27, Aleppo, 4 August 1860, PRO – FO, 78/1538.
TAYLOR, J.G. (British Consul). 'Report on Koordistan', 18 March 1869, PRO – FO, 78/2439.

PRINTED SOURCES

ARMENIAN PATRIARCHATE OF ISTANBUL. 'Azgayin Sahmanadruthiwn Hayots' (National Constitution of the Armenians), Istanbul, 1863.

124

'Teghekagirq gawarakan harstaharutheants' ('Report on the Outrages which Occurred in the Provinces'), Istanbul, 1876.
BRITISH GOVERNMENT. 'British and Foreign State Papers 1877-1878', vol.69, 1885.
BRYCE, J. (VISCOUNT). 'The Treatment of Armenians in the Ottoman Empire', 1916.
LEO (BABAKHANIAN, A.). 'Hayots hartsi vaweragrere' ('The Documents of the Armenian Question'), Tiflis, 1915.
NORADOUNGHIAN, G. (EFENDI). 'Recueil d'actes internationaux de l'Empire Ottoman', 4 vols, Paris-Leipzig-Neuchâtel, vol.1 (1300-1789), 1897; vol.2 (1789-1856), 1900; vol.3 (1856-78), 1902; vol. 4 (1878-1902), 1903.
OTTOMAN GOVERNMENT. 'Düstûr' ('Code of Laws'), Istanbul, vol.1, 1289H/1872-3; vol.2, 1289H/1872-3; vol.3, 1293H/1876; vol.4, 1299H/1881-2.
YOUNG, G. 'Corps de droit ottoman', 7 vols, Oxford, 1905-6.

OTTOMAN PROVINCIAL YEAR-BOOKS

ALEPPO ('Haleb vilâyeti salnamesi'): 1284H/1867-8; 1286H/1869-70; 1290H/1873-4; 1300H/1882-3; 1304H/1886-7; 1307H/1889-90; 1310H/1892-3; 1314H/1896-7; 1316H/1898-9; 1320H/1902-3; 1324H/1906-7 and 1326H/1908.
BEIRUT ('Beyrût vilâyeti salnamesi'): 1310H/1892-3; 1318H/1900-1; 1319H/1901-2 and 1326H/1908.
BITLIS ('Bitlîs vilâyeti salnamesi'): 1310H/1892-3; 1316H/1898-9; 1317H/1899-1900 and 1318H/1900-1.
DAMASCUS ('Sûriye vilâyeti salnamesi'): 1286H/1869-70; 1296H/1878-9; 1298H/1880-1; 1301H/1883-4; 1306H/1888-9; 1309H/1891-2; 1312H/1894-5; 1315H/1897-8 and 1318H/1900-1.
DIYARBAKIR ('Diyârbakir vilâyeti salnamesi'): 1286H/1869-70; 1291H/1874-5; 1294H/1877; 1297H/1879-80; 1302H/1884-5; 1306H/1888-9; 1308H/1890-1; 1316H/1898-9; 1319H/1901-2 and 1323H/1905-6.
ELÂZIG ('Ma'mûret ül-azîz vilâyeti salnamesi'): 1298H/1880-1; 1300H/1882-3; 1302H/1884-5; 1305H/1887-8; 1307H/1889-90; 1308H/1890-1; 1310H/1892-3; 1312H/1894-5; 1321H/1903-4 and 1325H/1907-8.
ERZURUM ('Erzurûm vilâyeti salnamesi'): 1289H/1872-3; 1292H/1875; 1299H/1881-2; 1304H/1886-7; 1305H/1887-8; 1310H/1892-3; 1312H/1894-5; 1316H/1898-9 and 1318H/1900-1.
JABAL LUBNÂN ('Cebel-i Lübnân salnamesi'): 1304H/1886-7; 1305H/1887-8; 1306H/1888-9; 1307H/1889-90; 1308H/1890-1 and 1309H/1891-2.
SEYHAN ('Âdana vilâyeti salnamesi'): 1289H/1872-3; 1294H/1877; 1297H/1879-80; 1308H/1890-1; 1309H/1891-2; 1312H/1894-5 and 1319H/1901-2.
SIVAS ('Sîvâs vilâyeti salnamesi'): 1287H/1870-1; 1292H/1875; 1301H/1883-4; 1306H/1888-9; 1308H/1890-1; 1321H/1903-4 and 1325H/1907-8.
TREBIZOND ('Tarabzon vilâyeti salnamesi'): 1282H/1865-6; 1287H/1870-1; 1288H/1871-2; 1292H/1875; 1298H/1880-1; 1305H/1887-8; 1309H/1891-2; 1316H/1898-9; 1318H/1900-1 and 1322H/1904-5.

VAN ('Vân vilâyeti salnamesi'): 1315H/1897-8 (University Library of Istanbul, No.81042; Municipal Library of Istanbul, 'salnames', No. 34/1).

DICTIONARIES AND ENCYCLOPAEDIAS

CEVÂD, A.   'Memâliki osmâniyenin târîkh ve cogrâfyâ lugâti' ('Historical and Geographical Dictionary of the Ottoman Empire'), 4 vols, Istanbul, 1313-1317H (1895-1900).
'Encyclopaedia of Islam', 1st edn, 4 vols and supplement, Leiden-London, 1913-38; 2nd edn 1954-.
EPHRIKIAN, S.   'Bnashkharhik bararan' ('Armenian Geographical Dictionary'), Venice, vol.1 (2nd imp.), 1903-5; vol.2, 1907.
FRAŞERÎ, Ş.S. (BEY).   'Qâmûs ül-a'lâm' ('Dictionary of Proper Names'), 6 vols, 1306-1316H (1888-99).
'Islâm ansiklopedisi', Istanbul, 1950-.
'Türkiye ansiklopedisi', 6 vols, Ankara, 1956-8.

NEWSPAPERS AND PERIODICALS

'Handês amsoreay' (Monthly philological review of the Armenian Mkhitharist Fathers), Vienna, 1890, 1951 and 1968.
'The Journal of the Royal Asiatic Society', 1942.
'Masis' (Masis = 'Ararat', a daily newspaper), Istanbul, 1857-63.
'Mshak' ('Cultivator', a newspaper), Tiflis, 1878.
'S. Perkitch':   'Endardzak oratsoyts S. Perktchean hiwandanotsi' ('Large Almanac of the Armenian St Perkitch Hospital'), Istanbul, 1900-28.
'Revue des Études Arméniennes', vol.9 (1929).
'Surhandak' ('Courier', a newspaper), Istanbul, 1903.
'Taretsoyts 1914' (an almanac for the year 1914), Istanbul, published by the Trusteeship of the Armenian students.
THEODIK, 'Amênun taretsoytse' ('The Almanac for Everyone'), Istanbul, 1911, 1912, 1922.
'The Times', London, 1894-7.
TOLPAGIAN (DOLBAKIAN), E.   'Libanani patkerazard oratsoyts' ('Illustrated Almanac of the Armenians of Lebanon'), Beirut, 1936.

MAPS

Anatolia

(a) E. BOWEN, 'A New Accurate Map of Anatolia or Asia Minor with Syria and such other Provinces of the Turkish Empire as Border thereupon', 1747, size: 34.5 x 42 cm, scale: English miles 60 to a degree.
(b) H. KIEPERT, 'Neuer Hand-Atlas', Berlin, 1859/60 (2nd edn, 1881), copyright by Dietrich Reimer, table 27 'Kleinasien und Syrien', size: 54 x 43 cm, scale: 1 : 300,000.
(c) H. KIEPERT, C. GRÄF, A. GRÄF and C. BRUHNS, 'Handatlas der Erde und des Himmels' (Weimar, Geographical Institut), 1878, table 51

'Die asiatische Türkei, die Kaukasusländer und West Persien', size:
65.5 x 54 cm, scale: 1 : 3,600,000.
(d) The maps of various provinces of Anatolia by VITAL CUINET in his
'La Turquie d'Asie'.

Armenia

(a) S.T. EREMIAN, map to 'History of the Armenian People' (in
Armenian), Erevan, 1952.
(b) H. KIEPERT, 'Atlas antiquus', Berlin, copyright by Dietrich
Reimer, 1898 (2nd edn, 1902), table 5 'Asia Citerior', size: 42.5 x
33.5 cm, scale: 1 : 4,000,000.
(c) W.M. CALDER and G.E. BEAN, 'A Classical Map of Asia Minor',
London, 1958, size: 72 x 48 cm (28.5 x 19 in.), scale: 1 :
2,000,000.

Lebanon

'Lubnân' prepared by BÛLOS AWWÂD (Paul K. Aouad), printed in 1956 at
Paris (copyright by Girard, Barrière & Thomas), and published in
Beirut under the supervision of the Ministry of Education and Fine
Arts; size: 123 x 89 cm, scale: 1 : 160,000.

Syria

'al-Iqlîm al-Sûrî ('The Syrian Region of the United Arab Republic'),
prepared by ZIYA SHUKRI'L NA'AL, printed in 1959 at Groningen
(Netherlands) by Van Dingen and published in Aleppo under the supervision of the Ministry of Education; size: 104.5 x 80.5 cm, scale:
1 : 700,000.

OTHER PRINTED BOOKS

i. Works in Turkish

ÇARK, Y. 'Türk devleti hizmetinde Ermeniler, 1453-1953' ('The
Armenians in the Service of the Turkish State, 1453-1953'),
Istanbul, 1953.
DANIŞMEND, I.H. 'Izahli osmanli tarihi kronolojisi' ('Elucidated
Chronology of the Ottoman History'), Istanbul, vol.4, 1955.
ISKIT, S.R. 'Türkiye'de neşriyat hareketleri tarihine bir bakiş'
('A Historical Survey of Publishing Activities in Turkey'),
Istanbul, 1939.
KARAL, E.Z. 'Osmanli tarihi' ('Ottoman History'), vol.6 (1861-76),
Ankara, 1956.
KOÇAŞ, S. 'Tarih boyunca Ermeniler ve Türk-Ermeni ilişkileri' ('The
Armenians in History and Turkish-Armenian Relations'), Ankara, 1967.
TURKISH GOVERNMENT. 'Türkiye'de meskûn yerler kilavuzu' ('Gazeteer
of the Inhabited Places of Turkey'), published by the Ministry of
the Interior of Turkey, 2 vols, Ankara, vol.1, 1946; vol.2, 1947.

URAS, E.   'Tarihte Ermeniler ve Ermeni meselesi' ('The Armenians in
History and the Armenian Question'), Ankara, 1950.

ii.   Works in Arabic

KAYYÂLÎ, S. AL-.   'al-Adâb al-'arabî'l mu'âshir fi Sûriyya' ('Modern
Arabic Literature in Syria'), Cairo, 1959.
MRUEH, A.   'Assahâfa'l 'arabiyyah' ('The Arabic Press'), Beirut,
1961.
SHAYKHO, L.   'al-Adâb al-'arabiyyah fi'l qarn al-tâsi 'ashar'
('Arabic Literature in the Nineteenth Century'), 2nd imp., Beirut,
vol.2, 1926.
TARRÂZÎ, PH. DI (COUNT).   'Târîkh al-assahâfa'l 'arabiyyah'
('History of the Arabic Press'), 3 vols, Beirut, 1912-14.
ZAYDÂN, J.   'Mashâhîr al-Sharq' ('The Renowns of the East'), 2nd
imp., Cairo, n.d.
ZAYDÂN, J.   'Târîkh adâb al-lugha'l 'arabiyyah' ('History of the
Literature in Arabic Language'), 2nd edn, Cairo, vol.4, 1957.

iii.   Works in Armenian

A., M.   'Turqiayi Hayern ew irents dratsiner' ('The Armenians of
Turkey and their Neighbours'), Marseilles, 1890.
ADJARIAN, H.   'Qnnuthiwn Hamsheni barbari' ('Study of the Dialect of
Hamshen'), Erevan, 1947.
ADJEMIAN, H.   'Hayots Hayrik' ('Armenians' Father'), 2 vols, Tavriz,
1929.
AGHASI (GARABED THUR-SARKISIAN).   'Zeytun ew ir shurtchakanere'
('Zeytun and its Surroundings'), Beirut, 1968.
AKINIAN, N.   'Simeon dpri Lehatswoy ughegruthiwne' ('The Travel
Diary of the Scribe Simeon from Lwow'), Vienna, 1936.
ALBOYADJIAN, A.   'Azgayin Sahmanadruthiwn' ('The National Constitu-
tion'), in the year-book of the Armenian St Perkitch Hospital in
Istanbul, Istanbul, 1910.
ALBOYADJIAN, A.   'Patmuthiwn Eudokioy Hayots' ('History of the
Armenians in Tokat'), Cairo, 1952.
ALBOYADJIAN, A.   'Patmuthiwn hay gaghthakanuthean' ('History of the
Armenian Emigration'), Cairo, vol.1, 1941;   vol.2, 1955;   vol.3/i,
1961.
ALBOYADJIAN, A.   'Patmuthiwn Malatioy Hayots' ('History of the
Armenians in Malatya'), Beirut, 1961.
ALEXANDRIAN, A.   'Patmuthiwn akanawor qaghaqin Sebastioy ew
sahmanats nora' ('History of the Famous Town of Sivas and of its
Boundaries'), Venice, 1911.
ANETSI, S.   'Hawaqmunq i grots patmagrats' ('A Collection from His-
tory Books'), Etchmiadzin (Armenia), 1893.
ARDZRUNI, TH.   'Patmuthiwn tann Ardzruneats' ('History of the
Ardzruni Dynasty'), Tiflis, 1917.
BADALIAN, KH.   'Haykakan hartse San Stefanoyi paymanagrum ew Berlini
Kongresum 1878' ('The Armenian Question in the Treaty of San Stefano
and in the Congress of Berlin in 1878'), Erevan, 1955.
BAKHTIKIAN, S.   'Arapkir ew shurtchakayi giwghere' ('Arapkir and the
Surrounding Villages'), Beirut, 1955.

BALASANIAN, S.   'Patmuthiwn Hayots' ('History of the Armenians'),
Tiflis, 1890.
BARSAMIAN, M.   'Akn ew Aknetsiq' ('Egin and its Armenian Popula-
tion'), Paris, 1952.
BEJISHKIAN, M.   'Patmuthiwn Pontosi' ('History of Pontus'), Venice,
1819.
BERBERIAN, A.   'Patmuthiwn Hayots' ('History of the Armenians'),
Istanbul, 1871.
BOGHOSIAN, E.   'Karapet Artin Pasha Davudian, 1816-1873' (in
Armenian), Vienna, 1949.
BOGHOSIAN, H.M.   'Zeytuni Patmuthiwne, 1409-1921' ('A History of
Zeytun, 1409-1921'), Erevan, 1969.
BOGHOSIAN, Y.   'Hayastani ashkharhagruthiwn' ('A Geography of
Armenia'), Paris, 1952.
BOGHOSIAN, Y.P.   'Hadjini endhanur patmuthiwn' ('The General History
of Haçin'), Los Angeles, 1942.
CALUSTIAN, K.   'Marash kam Germanik ew heros Zeytun' ('Marash or
Germanicia and the Heroic Zeytun'), New York, 1934.
DASHIAN, Y.   'Hay bnaktchuthiwne Sew Dzovên mintchew Karin' ('The
Armenian Population from Black Sea to Karin'), Vienna, 1921. There
is a French translation of it by F. Macler, 'La Population
arménienne de la région comprise entre la Mer Noire et Karin',
Vienna, 1922.
DJIZMEDJIAN, M.   'Kharpert ew ir zawaknere' ('Harput and her Sons'),
Fresno-Venice, 1955.
DÔ, A.   'Vani, Bitlisi ew Erzurumi vilayetnere' ('The vilâyets of
Van, Bitlis and Erzurum'), Erevan, 1912.
ERAMIAN, H.   'Yushardzan Van-Vaspurakani' ('Memorial of Van-
Vaspurakan'), 2 vols, Alexandria, 1929.
EREVANIAN, K.   'Patmuthiwn Çarsancaki Hayots' ('History of the
Armenians of Çarsancak'), Beirut, 1956.
GABIKIAN, K.   'Eghernapatum Phoqun Hayots ew norin medzi mayraqagha-
qin Sebastioy' ('History of the Massacres of Lesser Armenia and of
its Great Capital Sivas'), Boston, 1924.
GANTZAKETSI, K.   'Patmuthiwn Hayots' ('History of the Armenians'),
Tiflis, 1909.
GHAPHANTSIAN, G.   'Urartui patmuthiwne' ('History of Urartu'),
Erevan, 1940.
GHAZARIAN, H.   'Arewmtahayeri sotsial-tntesakan ew qaghaqakan
katsuthiwne, 1800-1870' ('The Socio-economic and Political Situation
of West-Armenians, 1800-1870'), Erevan, 1967.
GHEVOND VARDAPET.   'Arshawanq Arabats i Hays' ('The Invasions of
Arabs into Armenia'), Paris, 1857.
HAYK (HAIG), V.   'Kharpert ew anor oskeghên dashte' ('Harput and her
Golden Plain'), New York, 1959.
HAYKAZ, A.   'Shabin Karahisar' ('History of the Armenians in
Şebinkarahisar'), New York-Beirut, 1957.
KAROYAN (GAROYAN), G.   'Medz egherni nahatak hay bjishknere' ('The
Martyred Armenian Doctors of the Great Massacre'), Boston-Venice,
1957.
KELESHIAN, M.   'Sis-matean' ('A Book on Sis'), Beirut, 1949.
KETCHIAN, P.   'Patmuthiwn surb Perktchi hiwandanotsin Hayots i
Kostandnupolis' ('History of St Perkitch Hospital of the Armenians
in Constantinople'), Istanbul, 1888.

KHANDJIAN, H. 'Ashkharhagruthiwn osmanean petuthean' ('A Geography of the Ottoman Empire'), Istanbul, 1912.

KHATCHADRIAN, A. 'Hayastani sepagrakan shurtchani qnnakan patmuthiwn' ('Critical History of the Cuneiform Period of Armenia'), Erevan, 1933.

KOMMAGENATSI (KASSUNI, E.). 'Philartos Haye' ('Philaretos the Armenian'), Aleppo, 1930.

MANANDIAN, Y. 'Hayastani glkhawor djanaparhnere' ('The Main Routes of Armenia'), Erevan, 1936.

MANANDIAN, Y. 'Qnnakan tesuthiwn hay joghovrdi patmuthean' ('A Critical Survey of the History of the Armenian People'), Erevan, vol.1, 1944; vol.2/i, 1957; vol.2/ii, 1960; vol.3, 1952.

MANANDIAN, Y. 'Tigran erkrorde ew Hrome' ('Tigran II and Rome'), Erevan, 1940.

MARKOSIAN, S. 'Arewmtahayuthean vidjake XIX. dari vertcherin' ('The Situation of the West Armenians towards the end of the Nineteenth Century'), Erevan, 1968.

MEDZOPHETSI, TH. 'Patmuthiwn Lang-Tamuray' ('History of Tamerlane'), Paris, 1860.

MEGUERDITCHIAN, T. 'Tigranakerti nahangi tchardere ew Kurderu gazanuthiwnnere' ('The Massacres of the Province of Diyarbakir and the Ferocities of the Kurds'), Cairo, 1919.

MEZBURIAN, A.N. 'Hay ew dzagumov hay bjishkner, 1688-1940' ('Armenian Doctors and Doctors of Armenian Origin, 1688-1940'), vol. 1 (1688-1864), Istanbul, 1950-4.

MICHAYEL ASORI (MICHAEL OF SYRIA). 'Jamanakagruthiwn' ('Chronicles'), Jerusalem, 1871.

MIRAKHORIAN, M.K. 'Nkaragrakan ugheworuthiwn i hayabnak gawars arewelean Tadjkastani' ('Descriptive Travel in the Provinces inhabited by Armenians in Eastern Turkey'), 3 vols, Istanbul, 1884-5.

MKUND, T. 'Amidayi ardzagangneru verakotchumn' ('Reminiscence of the Echoes of Amida'), Weehawken (New Jersey), vol.2, 1953.

NATHANIAN, B. 'Artosr Hayastani' ('The Tears of Armenia'), Istanbul, 1879.

NATHANIAN, B. 'Teghekagruthiwn endhanur vidjakin Sebastioy' ('Report on the General Diocese of Sivas'), Istanbul, 1877.

ORMANIAN, M. 'Azgapatum' ('History of the Armenian Nation'), 1st edn, vols 1 and 2, Istanbul, 1912-13; vol.3, Jerusalem, 1927.

OSKERITCHIAN, M. 'Zeytun albom' ('Zeytun Album'), 2nd edn, Beirut, 1961.

PHIRANIAN, N. 'Kharperti egherne' ('The Massacres of Harput'), Boston, 1937.

SAHAKIAN, A. 'Diwtsaznakan Urfa ew ir Hayordinere' ('The Heroic Urfa and her Armenian Sons'), Beirut, 1955.

SARAFIAN, K. 'Patmuthiwn Antepi Hayots' ('History of the Armenians of Antep'), 2 vols, Los Angeles, 1953.

SARKISIAN (SARGISIAN), B. 'Mayr tsutsak hayerên dzeragrats Matenadaranin Mkhithareants i Venedig' ('Catalogue of the Armenian Manuscripts of the Mkhitharist Library in Venice'), Venice, vol.1, 1914.

SARKSIAN (SARGSIAN), E. 'Turqian ew nra nuadjoghakan qaghaqakanuthiwne Andrkovkasum' ('Turkey and its Policy of Conquest in Transcaucasia'), Erevan, 1964.

SARUKHAN, A. 'Haykakan khndire ew Azgayin Sahmanadruthiwne

Turqiayum' ('The Armenian Question and the National Constitution in Turkey'), Tiflis, 1912.

SEMERDJIAN, M. 'Zeytuni antsealên ew nerkayên' ('From the Past and Present of Zeytun'), vol.1, Vienna, 1900.

SHNORHALI, N. 'Endhanrakan thughthq' ('General Letters of St Nerses the Graceful'), Jerusalem, 1871.

SÜRMEYAN, A. 'Tsutsak hayerên tzeragrats Halepi surb Qarasun Mankunq ekeghetswoy' ('Catalogue of the Armenian Manuscripts of the Church of Forty Martyrs in Aleppo'), vol.1, Jerusalem, 1935.

SÜRMEYAN, A. 'Mayr tsutsak hayerên tzeragrats Jerusalemi srbots Yakobeants vanqi' ('Catalogue of the Armenian Manuscripts of St James's Monastery in Jerusalem'), vol.1, Venice, 1948.

SÜRMEYAN, A. 'Patmuthiwn Halepi Hayots' ('History of the Armenians of Aleppo'), vol.3, Paris, 1950.

TAGHAWARIAN, Y. 'Azgabanuthiwn Sebastioy Tchadirdjian gerdastani' ('Genealogy of the Tchadirdjian Family in Sivas'), New York-Beirut, 1957.

TARONETSI, S. 'Patmuthiwn tiezerakan' ('General History'), St Petersburg (Leningrad), 1885.

TCHAMTCHIAN, M. 'Patmuthiwn Hayots' ('History of the Armenians'), 3 vols, Venice, 1784-6.

TCHARIK, GH. 'Karinapatum' ('A History of Karin'), Beirut, 1957.

TERZIAN, S.Y. 'Hadjini uthamseay diwtsaznamarte' ('The Eight Months of Heroic Resistance of Haçin'), 2nd imp., Buenos Aires, 1956.

TERZIAN, Y. 'Kilikioy aghête' ('The Calamity of Cilicia'), Istanbul, 1912.

THEODIK. 'Tip u tar' ('Type and Letter'), Istanbul, 1912.

THORGOMIAN, V.Y. 'Bjishk Doctor Servitchên Efendi' ('Doctor Servitchên Efendi'), Vienna, 1893.

THORGOMIAN, V.Y. 'Hay bjishkakan ardzanagrabanuthiwn' ('Armenian Medical Inscriptions'), Venice, 1931.

THUMAYAN, K. 'Patmuthiwn arewelean khndroy ew aratchnord haykakan hartsi' ('History of the Eastern Question and a Guide to the Armenian Question'), 2 vols, London, 1905.

URHAYETSI, M. 'Jamanakagruthiwn' ('The Chronicles of Matthew from Urha'), Etchmiadzin, 1898.

VAN-VASPURAKAN'S UNION (editors). 'Vaspurakan', Venice, 1930.

VARDAN VARDAPET. 'Hawaqumn patmuthean' ('A Historical Collection'), Venice, 1862.

VARJAPETIAN (VARJABEDIAN), S. 'Hayere Libanani mêtch' ('The Armenians in Lebanon'), Beirut, 1951.

YAKOBIAN, V.A. 'Manr jamanakagruthiwnner' ('Small Chronicles'), 2 vols, Erevan, 1951 and 1956.

YARUTHIWNIAN, H. 'Hayastan IX-XI darerum' ('Armenia during the IX-XI Centuries'), Erevan, 1959.

ZARDARIAN, V. 'Yishatakaran, 1512-1912' ('Memorials, 1512-1912'), 3 vols, 1910-12.

iv. Works in European languages

ABKARIUS, I. b. Y. 'The Lebanon in Turmoil: Syria and the Powers in 1860', trans. from the Arabic and annotated by J.F. Scheltema,

New-Haven-London-Oxford, 1920.
ADONTZ, N. 'Histoire d'Arménie', Paris, 1946.
AKANTS, G. 'History of the Nation of the Archers', trans. from the Armenian by R.P. Blake and R.N. Frye, Harvard, 1954.
BLISS, D. 'The Reminiscences' (of D. Bliss), New York, 1920.
CAHEN, C. 'Pre-Ottoman Turkey', London, 1968.
CEDRENUS, G. 'Annales' (I. Bekker's edition), Bonn, 1838-9.
CUINET, V. 'La Turquie d'Asie', 4 vols, Paris, 1890-4, alphabetical table, 1900.
CUINET, V. 'Syrie, Liban et Palestine', Paris, 1896.
DAVUD (PASHA), K.A. 'Histoire de la législation des anciens Germains', 2 vols, Berlin, 1845.
ENGELHARDT, E. 'La Turquie et le Tanzimat ou histoire des réformes dans l'Empire Ottoman de 1826 jusqu'à nos jours', Paris, vol.1, 1882; vol.2, 1884.
FARLEY, J.L. 'The Resources of Turkey', London, 1862.
GARSTANG, J. and GURNEY, O.R. 'The Geography of the Hittite Empire', London, 1959.
GROUSSET, R. 'Histoire de l'Arménie des origines à 1071', Paris, 1947.
GROUSSET, R. 'L'Empire du Levant' (2nd edn), Paris, 1949.
HALID, H. 'The Diary of a Turk', London, 1903.
HERTSLET, E. 'The Map of Europe by Treaty', 4 vols; vol.4 (1875-91), London, 1891.
HITTI, PH.K. 'Lebanon in History', London-New York, 1957.
HOLLAND, TH.E. 'The European Concert in the Eastern Question', Oxford, 1885.
JESSUP, H.H. 'Fifty-three Years in Syria', 2 vols, New York-London, 1910.
JONQUIÈRE, LA. 'Histoire de l'Empire Ottoman' (2nd edn), Paris, 1914.
KÖPRÜLÜ, M.F. 'Les Minorités en Turquie', Strasbourg, 1936.
KORTEPETER, C.M. 'Ottoman Imperialism during the Reformation: Europe and the Caucasus', New York, 1972.
LÉART, M. (ZOHRAB/ZOHRAP, K.). 'La Question Arménienne à la lumière des documents', Paris, 1913.
LEHMANN-HAUPT, C.F. 'Armenien einst und jetzt', vol.1, Berlin, 1910; vol.2/i, Berlin-Leipzig, 1926; vol.2/ii, Berlin-Leipzig, 1931.
LEPSIUS, J. 'Der Todesgang des armenischen Volkes', Potsdam, 1919.
LEPSIUS, J. 'Deutschland und Armenien, 1914-1918', Potsdam, 1919.
LEWIS, B. 'The Emergence of Modern Turkey', London-New York-Toronto, 1961.
LYNCH, H.F.B. 'Armenia: Travels and Studies', 2 vols, London, 1901.
MANANDIAN, Y. (YAKOB/HAKOB). 'Tigrane II et Rome', trans. from the Armenian by H. Thorosian, Lisbon, 1963 (I have used the Armenian original work).
MARRIOTT, J.A.R. 'The Eastern Question', 4th edn, London, 1956.
MICHAYELIAN, G.G. 'Istoria Kilikiyskovo Armianskovo gosudarstva' ('History of the Armenian State of Cilicia'), Erevan, 1952.
MINORSKY, V. 'Hudûd al-'âlam' ('The Regions of the World'), an anonymous Persian treatise on geography (372H/962), Oxford, 1937.
MORGAN, J. DE. 'Histoire du peuple arménien', Paris, 1919.

NALBANDIAN, L.   'The Armenian Revolutionary Movement', University of California Press, Berkeley and Los Angeles, 1963.

NANSEN, F.   'L'Arménie et le Proche Orient', Paris, 1928.

ORMANIAN, M.   'The Church of Armenia', 2nd English edn, London, 1955.

PASDERMADJIAN, H.   'Histoire de l'Arménie', Paris, 1949.

PEARS, E. (SIR).   'The Life of Abdul Hamid', London, 1917.

PLUTARCH.'Lucullus' in 'Plutarch's Lives', 5 vols, trans. A.H. Clough, London, n.d.

RICHTER, J.   'A History of Protestant Mission in the Near East', London, 1910.

SANDALGIAN, J.   'Histoire documentaire de l'Arménie', 2 vols, Rome, 1917.

SARKISSIAN, A.O.   'History of the Armenian Question to 1885' (University of Illinois, 'Bulletin', vol.22, Nos 2 and 4), Urbana, 1938.

SARKISSIAN, A.O.   Concert Diplomacy and the Armenians, 1890-1897, in 'Studies in Diplomatic History and Historiography' (in honour of G.P. Gooch, edited by A.O. Sarkissian), Longmans, 1961, pp.48-75.

SAUVAGET, J.   'Alep: essai sur le développement d'une grande ville syrienne des origines au milieu du XIXème siècle' (Bibliothèque archéologique et historique), Paris, 1914; second volume, illustrations.

SCHLECHTA-WSSEHRD, O. DE.   'Manuel terminologique français-ottoman', Vienna, 1870.

SCHOPOFF, A.   'Les Réformes et la protection des chrétiens en Turquie, 1673-1904', Paris, 1904.

STRABO.   'The Geography' (in the Loeb Classical Library), with an English trans. by H.L. Jones, 8 vols, London-New York, 1917-32.

TACITUS.   'The Annals' (in the Loeb Classical Library), with an English trans. by J. Jackson, in 'The Histories and the Annals', London-Cambridge (Mass.), 1931 (reprinted 1943).

UBICINI, M.A.   'Letters on Turkey', trans. from the French by E. Easthope, in two parts, London, 1956.

WORTABED, J.   'Researches into the Religions of Syria' (drawn from original sources), London, 1860.

INDEX

AN EXPLANATORY NOTE TO THE INDEX

The most difficult problem in writing historical studies about a
certain country in a foreign language, is the question of
transliterating the names. I have solved the problem of geographical names of Eastern Anatolia in adopting the renderings as
given in the official 'Gazetteer of the Inhabited Places of Turkey'.
In the case of the province of Syria I followed a reasonable way of
transliteration, without crowding the text with diacriticals. I
have done the same with historical Arabic, Seljuk, Mongol and
Persian names. It was more problematic the presentation of Armenian
names in Latin characters. A classical transliteration, as I had
done in my original MS, looks rather odd and not very practical; a
consistent transliteration on a phonetic system would also cause
contradictions and confusions. In fact the East Armenian dialect
has retained the classical pronunciation, whereas the West Armenian
has lost the fineness of the stops (the mute consonant sounds) and
of affricates, still preserving the characters of this third
category. Therefore I chose a middle way: in many cases I
preferred the classical form, but in brackets gave the modern West
Armenian pronunciation. Only a few names appear in three different
transliterations. I was obliged to do so, because in the Armenian
Diaspora practically the same name is rendered in various forms;
for instance 'Karabet' (classical) usually is pronounced and
transliterated as 'Garabed', but sometimes also as 'Karabet', like
Mr Sarkis 'Karabet'ian (Vienna). I hope I have succeeded in solving
the problems of transliteration in a way which will seem satisfactory and acceptable to the most of my readers.
    I have divided the Index in three parts: 1. Personal names;
2. Place names; and 3. Important topics. Excluded are names of
nations, like Greek, Armenian, Turk, etc., and of places, such as
Anatolia (Eastern Anatolia), or Turkey or Armenia, which occur very
often.

INDEX OF PERSONAL NAMES

INDEX OF PLACE NAMES

INDEX OF IMPORTANT TOPICS